The Seven Layers of Integrity®

by

George P. Jones and
June Ferrill, Ph.D.

authorHOUSE™

1663 LIBERTY DRIVE, SUITE 200
BLOOMINGTON, INDIANA 47403
(800) 839-8640
WWW.AUTHORHOUSE.COM

First published by AuthorHouse 2/14/2006

ISBN: 1-4208-6684-2 (sc)

Library of Congress Control Number: 2005905629

Printed in the United States of America
Bloomington, Indiana

This book is printed on acid-free paper.

The Seven Layers of Integrity® is a registered trademark of ChangeMakers, Inc.

www.change-makers.com

Table of Contents

Preface

After an incredible, booming economy that lasted most of the last decade of the last century, America stumbled. The technology mania became a flash in history, the portfolios of soon to retire boomers turned to mush; and now we know that some of the rosiest corporate stories were complete fiction. From Enron to Worldcom to HealthSouth, earnings were manipulated or created, not earned – a manufacturing process that required the actions of executives in some of America's most well-known corporations.

Business schools across the land are wondering how they can keep from admitting the next corporate criminal. They are actively double-checking applicants' job histories, grade point averages and places of birth to see if they can spot falsehoods on the application.

When we first created the concept behind this book, we searched the Internet for training and literature on business ethics. At the time, we were focused on developing a training program, not a book. As we launched search after search we observed two things about the type of material already available. First, nearly all of the courses were based on theoretical treatments. Secondly, we observed that much of the material had been developed before the great boom of the nineties and the subsequent collapse.

It seemed to us that a more meaningful approach was truly needed.

There are several things that you will find about this book that differentiate it from others on the subject:

1. We don't start with Plato. In other words, this book is not based on the philosophical theory of ethics. If you are looking for that kind of treatment, this is not your source.

2. Our examples of behavior, good and bad, are taken directly from recent events. We refer to news you can relate to and discuss the challenges facing ordinary people in the first decade of the new millennium.

3. Most important, we don't assume that it is too late for adults to acquire improved values and a good sense of ethics. In this book we assume that most Americans in the workplace want to do what is right, but they don't always know what that means. We will take on the challenge of contemporary American business behavior and provide practical ways for people to form appropriate judgments about behavior and activity. We provide frames of reference to use in a practical manner when asking the question, "Is this something I should be doing?"

4. We use those same frames of reference, The Seven Layers of Integrity®, to provide even seasoned executives with additional points of view that may enable them to understand why legal behavior is not always sufficient and why the general public may view perfectly legal activity as unethical.

Of course, there are people in every walk of life that are unscrupulous, even criminal in their behavior. These people can be taught as well, in a special school called the justice system. We make no excuses for them.

On the other hand, our legal system and ways of doing business have become enormously complex. There are many questions that even the experts don't know how to answer. How then, can the average worker know what to do? It is our belief that some basic education, which is the purpose of this book and a related training program, will assist ordinary people in making the right judgment when called upon to do so. Basic education about professional codes of ethics, the importance of formal contracts, the legal concepts of agency and fiduciary, the political communities in which events play out and much more will help them to know when they should seek help in developing an answer.

As we wrote the first draft of this introduction, Sandy Weill had replaced the head of Salomon Smith Barney with a Citigroup corporate attorney and Jack Welch had decided that he should repay General Electric for some of the retirement "perquisites" he was going to get for free. Investors are still conservative about putting money back into stocks and the nation's economy is still suffering malaise, well into 2005.

Now is the time for our country to rediscover integrity and ethical behavior, not only in the business world but in every aspect of our individual and collective lives. In order to do so, we need re-education, for the world at large has taught us some very deceiving lessons over the past several decades.

This book is our attempt to begin that process.

On a personal note, many thanks are due to our spouses, families and friends who have encouraged us over the several years we worked together on this book. In particular we would like to thank Bob Knauss and Larry Hampton for their reviews and recommendations on the early drafts of this work.

George P. Jones
June Ferrill, Ph.D

Introduction

What is ethical behavior?

Most Americans probably believe they know the answer to this question. However, the truth is that this question has been the subject of thoughtful analysis by philosophers from the time of the ancient Greeks and lacks a simple answer. Perhaps that is because the question begs a circumstance – a specific situation or case example – in order to have an answer.

For example, is it ethical to kill a living creature? Some people believe that any creature, even an insect, should not be deliberately killed. Some believe that cows embody the reincarnated souls of human beings and should be protected. Some people believe that it is unethical to allow an injured or diseased animal to suffer, preferring to put the animal to sleep. There is a contemporary debate over allowing human beings to end their lives in similar circumstances. Is that ethical?

The subject of business ethics in particular has come to the forefront of discussion as a result of our most recent wave of fraudulent financial activity, misleading financial statements and conflicts of interest in the investment advisory community. A part of that discussion is focused on questions such as:

- Should business ethics be taught in our nation's M.B.A. schools?

- Can you really teach people to behave ethically?

These are clearly important questions, particularly to someone who undertakes to write a book on business ethics and integrity. The reader of such a book deserves an answer before proceeding further.

The issue of teaching business ethics in our M.B.A. programs and other business curricula is a very appropriate topic for national discussion. We are concerned, however, that this discussion may be approached as if ethics were mathematics or physics. For some people the desire to teach business ethics is really the desire to convey some specific laundry list of "Dos and Don'ts" to degree candidates and send them on their way into the world. As our introductory example regarding the question of killing living creatures would indicate, even the most basic and fundamental ethical behavior question does not readily lend itself to black and white answers.

This is not to say that college curricula should not convey the basic standards of business behavior. It can and should - indeed must - do so. But our expectation that such a course will somehow cover all one needs to know is unrealistic. There are as many ethical dilemmas available to the human race as there are actions and activities that the human race can undertake.

It is therefore imperative that we teach people how to *think*, not what to do. We need to convey an understanding of how to approach and resolve the day-to-day questions of ethical behavior in a business setting. A part of that understanding is certainly the existing body of knowledge on the subject, including existing standards of behavior. In particular, the codes of ethics of the various professions, the subject of a later chapter, should be one of the standards that are taught.

But in addition to that existing body of knowledge, business people should have a process to use when encountering new territory, a model that helps to clarify their thinking and a basic understanding of how to both recognize and resolve ethical problems in business operations.

That is the objective of this book.

The second question, "Can you really teach people to behave ethically?" has been posed to us by several business executives. We must admit struggling with this question at first, but we now have a clear resolve as to the answer: "YES!"

To explain our reasoning, we must first examine why people often raise this question. One body of thought is that by the time people reach adulthood their value systems are already in place and they are somehow either ethical or not ethical. This is classic contemporary American thinking characterized by binary, mutually exclusive options; sound bite readiness; and an implied potential for a litmus test on degree candidates or job applicants. As with most ideas having these characteristics, it falls apart under even limited scrutiny.

The answer lies in corporate culture. And the firmness of our resolve lies in the authors' own familiarity, after years of business consulting, with the impact of corporate culture on human behavior.

To illustrate the argument we will use two examples – one negative and one positive.

The negative example is the United States Air Force Academy in Colorado. The Academy came into the news (March 2003) as an investigation was underway into alleged rapes of female cadets by male upperclassmen on campus. As the investigation began, it appeared that this activity had been going on for a number of years – a timeframe that spanned the administrations of several Academy Directors. The problem most likely originated when women were first allowed to join men at the Academy and train to become officers in the United States Air Force.

The U.S. military academies have a prestige within the U.S. military, a prestige that originated with West Point and continued with the U.S. Naval Academy in Annapolis and the more recently founded Air Force Academy. Competition to get into these schools is stiff. The young men and women who get into West Point, Annapolis and Colorado Springs must meet a number of high standards with respect to academic work, physical ability and character. It is often necessary to be recommended by a member of Congress as part of the application process.

In short, if there were any place in which we would expect applicants to have highly scrutinized records, background checks and strong personal references, it would be in these fine institutions that create future generations of military leaders.

Somewhere along the way, a number of these young men of character, the finest in their local communities, allegedly became criminals. We say criminals because rape is a crime in all fifty states. And they did so in a relatively short time (two years, if the alleged rape was committed in one's junior year) and in the presence of an establishment that teaches discipline and obedience and where all of one's colleagues are also outstanding young men of character in their communities.

How did this happen? A strong part of the answer lies in the culture of the institution itself. We should not be surprised that the investigation's report used the word *culture* and recommended changes in that culture. Institutional culture, corporate culture if you will allow, made the intimidation of male and female cadets an expected part of behavior. In the case of female cadets, that intimidation took some very ugly turns. But the culture did not stop there. According to some reports, female officer candidates were told not to report incidents of rape. Those who did report them quickly found the system turned on them instead of on their attacker. Many of these women dropped out of the Academy. As for the attackers, one can only speculate, but one speculation is that the culture actually rewarded their behavior in some way, if only through an enhanced reputation for toughness in an institution in which toughness has a legitimate value.

The lesson to be learned is this: people who were essentially ethical when they arrived were quickly trained to either commit clearly unethical acts or to at least look the other way when their colleagues committed them. They were trained by an institutional culture that had a legitimate system of rewards and punishments that became somewhat out of control.

The above paragraph can be equally well applied to Enron, a company one of us consulted with twice during his career and where we both had many friends and business acquaintances. Corporate culture can train outstanding young people from fine families, communities and universities to commit unethical acts and even outright crimes, either aware or unaware, and to look the other way when others commit them. It can actively work to push the whistle blower out the door and to reward those who did so.

So we know people can be corrupted. Can the reverse be true? We need to be careful here to avoid an incorrect statement of what the reverse argument is. The reverse argument is not "Can unethical people be trained to be ethical?" The reverse argument is "Can a diverse group of young adults, most with a basic moral compass of right and wrong, be trained to behave in a superior professional manner, one that is not only ethical but exemplary?"

The answer is "YES!" And it takes a corporate culture that clearly supports ethical behavior and personal excellence.

Now the reader may well ask, "What is an example of such a fine company and how can I go to work there?"

There are actually many such companies across America. And there are many more that could be. Every company has its culture. Indeed, every company has at least two – its espoused culture and its real culture. The espoused culture is the one that is official. It includes the company's mission statement, its vision statement, its corporate values and many similarly named items. They are usually displayed on conference room walls, reception areas and executive desks. Then there is the real culture. The real culture is what people actually get rewarded and punished for. Real culture is similar to peer pressure among teenagers – it is brutal and in your face every day you are there. Most of us quickly learn to adapt to the real culture or at least keep a low profile when we disagree. Those that want to ride to the top learn how to actively embrace and promote the real culture in all aspects of their daily lives. Real culture can vary from department to department and location to location, but it always follows rewards and punishments.

Imagine being the one male cadet at the Academy who raises his hand and says: "This is wrong!" That is the impact of real culture.

So where are the good companies?

Thomas Watson, Sr. became the General Manager of the three-year old Computing Tabulating Recording Company in 1914. At first the company manufactured the office equipment of the day including clunky old typewriters. At the end of World War II, Watson was introduced to the computer – a massive assemblage of vacuum tubes and wires. For some reason, Watson decided to make a few, even though, as legend has it, he never believed he could sell more than a handful of them.

As with most companies that have grown under the leadership of a strong personality, IBM quickly developed its own culture following the persona of that leader.

As IBM grew, it opened manufacturing plants up and down the Hudson River Valley. It also started making a new electric typewriter with a marching ball that flipped around and something called a transistor based computer.

Years later, Thomas Watson, Jr. replaced his father and computers were being manufactured as fast as possible. IBM at that time was at its peak. The computers were being made for companies with recognizable names from all across America: General Electric, Boeing, Pan Am and many others.

The espoused values at IBM were represented at that time by an important sign on the desk of every manager. It had three lines that summarized these principles:

Respect for the Individual
Customer Service
Quality Work

These were the espoused values of Thomas Watson, Sr. and of his company. Note that "Respect for the Individual" came first.

The Watsons had managed to make the company's real culture match its espoused culture. IBM was known for a long time as an excellent place to work, a place where bright people could not only excel but were provided with a constant stream of in-house training to improve their skills. A separate research facility in Yorktown, just outside Manhattan, hired Ph.D.s in many fields and gave them the money to pursue their interests. Similar to AT&T's Bell Labs, the IBM R&D facility cranked out countless patents and advanced the physical and other sciences in ways we will never hear about.

Of course the company's culture also took on some unhealthy characteristics of insularity and bureaucracy to the point where an outsider, Lou Gerstner, had to be brought in to fix things. Gerstner did an excellent job by all reports and IBM remains today one of the best places in the country to work. The company has an excellent track record in business ethics, particularly given its overall scale and scope of operations.

So our answer to the question "Can you really train people to behave ethically?" is a resounding "YES!" The fact is that we train people to behave in many different ways in companies, in government, in non-profit organizations, schools, universities and all walks of life. We do that every single day all across our nation. We do it through real corporate culture and the related system of rewards and punishments.

We believe companies can train people to have a greater focus on the ethical implications of what they decide and what they do. We further believe people can even be trained to behave in ways that become exemplary standards of professionalism and community values. All it takes is focus.

Chapter One – The Seven Layers of Integrity®: Overview

When we began considering how to teach people about ethical behavior in business, we were immediately faced with a key question: What is ethical behavior?

Indeed, what is integrity? We often use words thinking we know what they mean and that everyone has the same interpretation as ours. It is always useful to consult a dictionary and examine the standard meanings.

Integrity is typically given three definitions in a dictionary. One is as a synonym for honesty. Someone with integrity is honest and/or sincere.

Integrity is also related to the word *integer*, which is a mathematical term that stands for the set of whole numbers: 1, 2, 3, and so on. Integrity, therefore, also carries the meaning of wholeness, or completeness. It is a characteristic of integers that they are mathematically complete.

A person of integrity, therefore, is not only honest and sincere, but also whole and complete – the second definition provided by the dictionary. In the common vernacular one might call such a person "a person of character." Someone whose behavior is consistently honest in all aspects of life, including family, business, community and spirituality, has integrity.

A third definition for integrity focuses specifically on ethics. Integrity is the quality of being of sound moral principle, adhering to a code or standard of values. Combining this definition with the definition of wholeness and completeness, we come to understand that a person of integrity adheres to her standard of values across all aspects of life. We expect persons of integrity to have that characteristic within their families and to exhibit it in the business world as well.

The word *ethical*, as a description of behavior, is very similar to this last definition of integrity. Ethics itself is a field of study, the focus being standards of conduct and moral codes or values. *Ethical* carries the definition of "conforming to the standards of conduct of a given profession or group." (1)

The concepts of ethical behavior and integrity are closely related. In essence, ethical behavior consistently follows the code or standards of a group of people. In some cases, such as a marriage, that group could be as few as two. In the case of our own inner spiritual values it may be a group of one – our Self.

Therefore, the definition of what constitutes ethical behavior, particularly in business and professional situations, varies depending upon the specific standards of the group that is evaluating the behavior. Because there are always many groups involved in evaluating business behavior, many different standards are applicable in that evaluation. For example, a refinery is subject to legal and regulatory standards, but may also be judged by local community expectations and the higher moral value of preservation of the environment for future generations.

These differing standards are the rules upon which others make judgments about our behavior. We have identified and categorized different groups and their standards into seven sets, which comprise a model we call The Seven Layers of Integrity®. Each layer is intended to represent a perspective you can apply in evaluating the ethical characteristics of business behavior. This model is represented in Diagram 1.

These seven perspectives take us from the lowest common denominator – obeying the law – to the highest and most demanding level – spiritual values that call upon us to continually grow, develop and reach outside ourselves to unselfishly help the most remote stranger.

The First Layer – The Law

In explaining and using The Seven Layers of Integrity® model, we start with the one ethical standard for business and professional behavior that most of us can agree with: any business activity that breaks the law is unethical. This is the absolute minimum requirement of an orderly civilization based on democracy, capitalism and the rule of law.

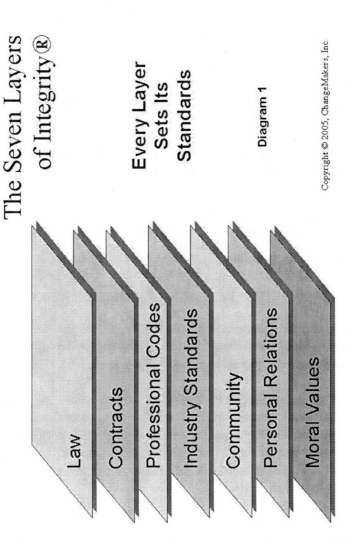

The Seven Layers of Integrity®

Every Layer Sets Its Standards

Law
Contracts
Professional Codes
Industry Standards
Community
Personal Relations
Moral Values

Diagram 1

Copyright © 2005, ChangeMakers, Inc.

Although many people advocate that the foundation of ethics consists of spiritual and moral values, we start with the law because we can all agree that the law represents an irrefutable standard for ethical *business and professional* behavior.

If we began our discussion with spiritual and moral values, we would immediately lose those people who don't acknowledge a spiritual realm. We would also have to tackle the issue of "Whose spirituality or morality is the 'right' one?"

Therefore, the best starting point for a practical discussion of ethical business and professional behavior is the law.

The Second Layer - Contracts and Agreements

Closely related to the law are the contracts and agreements that a business has with other parties. The standard presented in the second layer requires that a company adhere to the terms of a contract or agreement.

Contracts and agreements have a basis in the law. Indeed, the main purpose of civil law is to provide a basis for enforcement of contracts. In many ways, a contract is essentially an extension of the law.

Nonetheless, contracts and agreements are categorized in our model as a distinct layer from the law, because the groups setting the related standards are different. In the case of the law, the groups that set the standards are the legislative branches of our various governmental bodies; in the case of contracts, the parties to the agreement have set the rules that apply to their behavior.

Not all contracts are made in writing, but even verbal agreements have some basis in the law and are potentially enforceable. Regardless, a strong sense of business ethics should lead people to do their very best to uphold contracts and agreements, to deal with necessary changes to them in an open and fair manner, and to honor commitments made on behalf of the company.

The Third Layer – Professional Codes of Ethics

Many Americans work in a profession as engineers, doctors, accountants, and psychologists, for example. The professions have professional standards and codes of ethics that apply to anyone engaged in that profession. These professional standards and codes of ethics are separate and apart from any company or industry that employs the professionals.

The formal codes of ethics of the various professions have many common elements that are useful in examining and analyzing the ethical attributes of any business behavior, including the behavior of people who are not members of a formal profession.

The Fourth Layer – Industry Standards

In the chapter on industry standards, we will turn our attention to the business environment – the industry in which the business operates. Every industry has its rules and we will explore the implications of these typically unwritten standards of behavior.

Industry standards are important, but are often not backed by the force of law or a licensing organization. Violations of industry standards may or may not invoke penalties. It is also possible that industry standards conflict with the law, in which case the law should clearly rule. We will explore these issues in discussing this layer.

The Fifth Layer – The Community

No company or profession operates in a vacuum. We are all part of a greater community, be it local, national, or global. Some companies are particularly involved with communities such as the "investing public" or the "health care consumer." We will explore the implications for ethical behavior in the context of these communities and their standards or expectations for behavior.

The Sixth Layer – Personal Relationships

The last two layers are more focused on the individual.

The perspective of family and personal relationships provides additional views of what constitutes right and wrong. Some of those views have implications for the workplace and become relevant in how people interact on the job. How we treat others, particularly those with whom we have business and professional relationships, is definitely a business ethics issue.

The Seventh Layer – Moral and Spiritual Values

Finally, we turn to spiritual and moral values. As already noted, often this realm is the most difficult area for Americans to explore together. We will examine how these perspectives can be used to assist in analyzing the ethical behavior of businesses and business people.

After discussing each layer in detail, we will return to the model and compare and contrast the layers. We will then focus on current issues related to ethical business behavior, including recent sources of business litigation, issues concerning corporate culture and the challenges of electronic communication. We will use examples from current events to explore these issues.

Our goal is to help you learn how to navigate treacherous waters in your own life, discuss how individuals can have a positive ethical impact in their companies and identify places and times where you need to consult with others.

Footnotes

(1) *Webster's New World Dictionary of the American Language,* Second College Edition, William Collins and World Publishing Co., Inc., 1976.

Chapter Two – The First Layer of Integrity: The Law

The Importance of Law and Its Role

Every underdeveloped country trying to adopt capitalism struggles to clear one important hurdle: establishing the rule of law.

The sanctity of the rule of law is vital to our success as a free enterprise economy. The law, the ability to enforce the law and the deliberate, methodical attempt to apply the law equitably ("Blind Justice") provide the grease on which our economic engine relies.

Without the existence of law and its enforcement by the government, reliable contracts and investments cannot be made; and people lacking power and the tools of corruption cannot accumulate wealth. The laws related to business have a fundamental purpose: to enable contracts to exist and to be subject to the interpretation and enforcement of the courts.

The establishment of a government of law (based on a constitution) versus a government of men (based on kings, rulers, or despots) provides a more reliable environment in which business can operate. The ability to enter into and rely on written contracts and agreements reflects the nation's adherence to the rule of law. The ability to rely on contracts assists companies legally acquiring capital, making investments possible. Contracts also assist companies in predicting cash flow, another fundamental component of sound investment decisions.

Written, enforceable contracts decrease the risk associated with significant business transactions. Reduced business risk assists in more effectively allocating resources (materials, processes and personnel) because a corporation can better predict the outcome of its resource utilization. This promotes operational efficiency, which in turn creates wealth.

The rule of law, therefore, is absolutely essential to the United States' economy and is instrumental in the generation of wealth for individual citizens. The law, therefore, plays an important part in the improvement of our population's general standard of living. For example, people who live in the poorest parts of our inner cities have access to indoor plumbing because our nation's overall wealth provided the necessary plumbing and sewage infrastructure.

The former Soviet Union provides an illustration of what can happen when the rule of men overcomes the rule of law. The communist economy of the U.S.S.R. was stronger than the Russian economy of the late nineties following the fall of the Soviet Union.

The reason for this weakness was not that Russians didn't know how to make capitalism work. The reason was the failure of the rule of law. People were being shot in the streets in open gang warfare. Corruption and extortion were rampant. Money was being yanked out of newly formed companies and deposited in Swiss bank accounts, threatening a halt to foreign investing.

After Vladimir Putin focused his efforts on restoring law and order, his nation's economy moved forward, the situation began improving and foreign investors renewed their interest.

The rule of law is vital to economic activity in a democratic capitalist society. The law provides three basic support structures for our private enterprise system: the recognition and protection of private property; the recognition and enforcement of contracts; and remedy for injury caused by another party. Our nation's legal system has been the envy of the world and has been a factor in our ability to grow our economy, create wealth, retain domestic capital, attract foreign capital and ultimately improve our lives.

Unfortunately, a number of significant fraudulent financial activities were exposed in 2001 and 2002. Executive level personnel and company officers of Enron, TYCO and MCI were indicted. Stock values of these and other companies collapsed. Investors and retirees became anxious about their portfolios.

Fraudulent financial statements caused great financial injury to many individual investors, pension funds, banking institutions and workers. Some people lost their jobs, their medical benefits and their retirement funds in a single event. Filing false financial statements with the Securities and Exchange Commission is a crime. When the law is violated, significant economic damage can occur.

The Categories of Law

Law is classified into civil and criminal. Through criminal law, the government attempts to protect its citizens from crime. Criminal law may impose fines, penalties and restrictions on business activity, and its enforcement may result in incarceration.

Civil law enables the courts to protect one individual or organization from another by protecting established rights and enforcing contracts. Violations of civil law generally do not result in jail sentences, but can result in significant financial, business and professional consequences.

Law, Regulation and Business Operations

Business in the United States is subject to a host of laws from a variety of levels of government and agencies of government. The same is true for any person who establishes a small business, whether the business is organized as a small company or simply as an individual "doing business as" (DBA).

State Law

Businesses are organized and chartered under the law of a state. The states are the first and primary creators, promulgators and enforcers of business law.

Within the context of state law, companies may organize, establish themselves, enter into a banking relationship, issue shares of stock (privately) to investors in exchange for capital, establish a location, enter into written agreements to conduct business with other parties (companies or individuals) and submit to a state court for the resolution of disputes.

Under state law, companies hire employees and pay state unemployment taxes. The employment agreements between companies and employees are subject to state law, as is the treatment of employees by companies. States may define regulations governing the workplace environment.

States may also regulate specific industries. State industry regulations may govern worker safety, job protection or the safety of the general public.

Certain professions and occupations may also be subject to state regulation. Accountants, doctors, lawyers and engineers are typically licensed to practice by the state in which they operate. State regulation may dictate educational requirements to be met both initially and on an on-going basis (Continuing Professional Education) in order to hold a license.

States also license various non-professional occupations such as beauticians, plumbers and electricians.

In short, state law and state level agencies oversee a long list of business activities in most states. For this reason, the New York State Attorney General has the authority to investigate Merrill Lynch, Salomon Smith Barney and the mutual funds industry. For the same reason, the Attorneys General of the fifty states were able to tackle big tobacco.

Local Law

Local, county and city or other municipal governments and their various agencies also enact laws that impact businesses and professionals.

Local law provides building and occupancy codes, fire regulations, some traffic regulations, and health code regulations. If you own a restaurant, local ordinances and food inspectors are important to you. Construction activities such as home building and commercial construction are regulated by local building codes. Occupancy permits, fire inspections and burglar alarm permits are examples of other common local business requirements.

Many local governments impose taxes on business and professionals. Such taxes can include an income tax, hotel room taxes and various fees applicable to specific industries and professions.

The penalties for breaking local laws are typically not severe and ordinarily consist of a fine. However, cities can also revoke your license. They can close a restaurant or beautician operation as a health risk; a bar, due to violations of the occupancy limitation; and an office building, because it is structurally unsafe.

Federal Law

Any business that crosses state lines is subject to federal law. Federal law also applies to employment activities, publicly held companies and specific industries such as the pharmaceutical industry, the food industry and the insurance industry.

Federal laws apply to a wide range of business activities. Most companies are under the jurisdiction of federal law in the following areas:

People

Federal Law applies to a broad range of employment activities. Companies and professionals need to be aware of the laws involving hiring and discrimination, as well as immigration law and the requirements of Federal income tax, Social Security and Medicare.

Financial Activity

Almost any corporate financial transaction is subject to federal law. Revenue must be reported in your income tax filing. If your business buys any type of asset – land, an office building, computers, furniture, office equipment, or another company – the company must report it on the company's income tax return. If a company is publicly held, SEC regulations play a significant role in reporting requirements. All expenses are reportable for income tax purposes. The Sarbanes-Oxley Act places significant requirements on publicly held companies and their executive officers in an attempt to improve the reliability and accuracy of corporate financial statements used by the investing public.

Business Operations

Any company that conducts business across state lines or through the mail is under federal jurisdiction (the Interstate Commerce

Act and U.S. Postal regulations, including those related to mail fraud are examples).

Other examples of areas involving federal laws include pollution control, employee safety, interstate commerce, international trade and conducting business with foreign companies (Foreign Corrupt Practices Act). Specific federal laws also govern certain industries, such as pharmaceutical manufacturing.

Nearly every company is subject to a wide range of complex rules and regulations that are the law of the land. They come from all levels: local, state and federal.

If we assume that obeying the law is the most basic measure of ethical business behavior, understanding which laws apply to your activities and undertaking the diligence of knowing those requirements is a fundamental step.

Recent examples of instances in which corporations allegedly strayed from adhering to the law include:

- The high-tech industry, particularly Internet based companies, grew at a very fast pace. There were a number of reported instances of potential legal violations by some of these companies, including failure to follow good hiring practices, a lack of documented sexual harassment policies and inadequate attention to rules governing employee termination.

- Texaco allegedly encountered problems when it came to following federal anti-discrimination practices. A tape recording made during a meeting in which management discussed employee promotions allegedly revealed discrimination against minority employees, and Texaco ended up settling the matter for many millions of dollars.

- Several major corporations including Enron, TYCO, MCI Worldcom, and HealthSouth have been charged with various allegations concerning the accuracy of their financial statements.

- Former executives of TYCO, Adelphia, MCI Worldcom, Enron, HealthSouth and many others were and are in legal trouble.

- Oscar Wyatt, founder and former Chairman of Coastal States Gas Producing Company, allegedly paid kickbacks to obtain contracts under the United Nations' Iraq Food for Oil program.

Obeying the law should always be a focus of attention. Every company owes this to its shareholders, not to mention the general public, customers and business partners. Every employee, from CEO to night watchman, should be aware of what the laws are that affect his day-to-day responsibilities. The first step in obeying the law is to know the law. That is both a corporate responsibility and an individual responsibility. It is the first step, the most basic step, on the road to ethical business behavior.

Chapter Three – The Second Layer: Contracts and Agreements

Formal Contracts

A formal contract is an agreement executed by two or more parties. The term *executed* means the agreement, in the form of a document, has been signed by executives or officers who have the authority to commit their organizations to such agreements.

A contract:

1. States the nature of the agreement, the responsibilities of each party, and the consideration (compensation, payment, or fees) that will be exchanged between them;

2. Documents the recourse available to each party if the other party violates the contract;

3. Establishes safeguards with respect to confidential information, trade secrets, employees, ownership of a common customer, and any other important matter; and

4. Identifies specific remedies if one of the parties breaks the contract.

State law provides the basis for business contracts. A state's courts have jurisdiction over the contract when both parties to the agreement are organized in that state. Otherwise, the contract should have a provision identifying the state that has jurisdiction. The contract may stipulate that the parties settle their differences through arbitration or mediation instead of trial.

Adhering to the terms of a formal contract is as fundamental to ethical business behavior as obeying the law. A contract becomes, in effect, a law between the parties to the agreement and can be legally enforced through the state courts. Deliberate contract violations can lead to significant financial and operational penalties. Financial penalties could involve paying the other party for damages, attorney fees and court costs. Operational penalties could include being served with an injunction, by the state, against certain activities – in effect being legally barred from conducting certain types of business for a period of time.

Bribery and Contracts

Before a contract can exist, companies seek to develop business relationships. Establishing such relationships usually requires social interaction, which is more important in some cultures than others. For example, Asian cultures demand that a relationship be established before trust can occur. Latin American cultures are much the same. Problems for American companies ensue when potential or existing clients expect entertainment and gift-giving. Questions arise as to what constitutes reasonable expenses and what constitutes bribery. The Foreign Corrupt Practices Act makes bribery illegal. The text of the law can be found on the Department of Justice web site:

http://www.usdoj.gov/criminal/fraud/fcpa/fcpastat.htm

Bribery, whether for establishing business in the U.S. or abroad, undermines the free market system and rewards companies who have money to buy business regardless of the suitability or merit of the products or services. However, it would be naïve to think that influence and relationships do not need to be established. The question to be answered is: what type of relationship building is appropriate and within the law? To some extent, gray areas exist, especially when a company does not have an established, written policy. When answering the question of appropriateness, you need to look at the following elements:

- What is the law (foreign and domestic)? U.S. law and state laws are particularly important if the recipient is a government employee. U.S. law and foreign law are important if the recipient's company is domiciled outside the United States. Consult your attorneys if you do not know the law.

- What is the company's policy? Every company should have written policies governing appropriate client entertainment and the value of gifts. Consult your human resources department or corporate counsel.

- What is the price being paid for entertainment or gifts? Check your company's policies first. If the company has no policies then consider how others could perceive the gift.

- What is the intention of the gift or entertainment? Entertainment for the purpose of relationship building is usually acceptable; entertainment for the purpose of influencing a contract decision is not.

- What is the acceptable practice within the industry? In the absence of specific laws or company policy, guidance can be derived from general practice in the industry.

- How is the gift or entertainment likely to be perceived by others? If you would be embarrassed by public disclosure of the gift or entertainment, then reconsider. If a competitor is likely to perceive the gift as buying influence, then the gift can become a problem.

Formal Contracts Shape the Relationship

Formal contracts often establish the overall business relationship between the parties. Provisions in the contract will dictate the ownership of intellectual property (for example, engineering drawings and designs, new technology and patents), processes for amending or terminating the agreement and processes for notification of potential schedule slippage and budget overruns. Other contract provisions may establish the quality of the product delivered or services rendered. Contracts also establish rules for communicating with external parties by prohibiting disclosure of the agreement, limiting the right to use the buyer's name in marketing material and requiring approval on other communications about the business arrangement.

In essence, the formal contract has a strong impact on the relationship between the parties.

Deliberate Contract Violations

Deliberate violations occur when one party to the contract willfully decides to violate some or all of the terms of the agreement. Deliberately violating a written agreement conveys the following messages:

- The formal word of the company itself and the executive(s) who signed the contract cannot be trusted.

- The company's executives and officers do not believe the law applies to them; they believe they can operate as they please.

- The company believes the other party's rights are inconsequential.

- The company believes the other party is not big enough or strong enough to protect its contractual rights.

Deliberate contract violations can lead to significant financial and operational penalties:

- Financial penalties could involve paying the other party for damages, attorney fees and court costs.

- Operational penalties could include being served with an injunction, by the state, against certain activities – in effect being legally barred from conducting certain types of business for a period of time.

Some companies still choose to willfully violate a formal contract despite the risk of financial and operational penalties. We illustrate this point with two examples from our own experience.

An information systems consulting company had a formal contract with a Fortune 500 conglomerate. Under the terms of the agreement, our consulting company supplied this client with a group of one hundred programmers to work on various projects. In exchange, our consulting company gave the client a steeply discounted hourly rate for the programmers.

A year later, the client began decreasing the number of programmers assigned to their business. The contract specified tiers of rates based on the number of programmers actually assigned. When the number dropped below seventy-five, the rate increased.

Our company notified the client that the new rate would be in effect. The client refused to pay the increase.

Following a number of meetings with the client's CIO, our company still could not get the client to agree to pay what the contract required. Finally, we suggested that they ask their external counsel to review the contract, because we were thinking of going to court.

Two weeks later, in a meeting at their external counsel's offices, we were told that the contract was clear and our client would pay the difference – an amount of approximately a million dollars.

This was a successful outcome and illustrates some of the options that are available in a dispute. First discuss the problem, then try to negotiate a mutually acceptable amendment to the agreement, then threaten legal action, and finally, as a last resort, take legal action. But this example also illustrates how readily an otherwise reputable organization might willfully choose to violate a contract.

Another incident from our own experience involved a large publicly held company in the Northeast. This client retained a consulting firm to develop a state of the art system for customer order processing. A few months before the project was to complete, a very successful pilot was conducted at one of their facilities. At the same time, the customer's executive in charge of our work, who had executed the contract, was replaced. His replacement, hired from outside the organization, immediately brought the work on the project to a halt.

That in itself was not an ethical problem. Contracts can be terminated, and, when they are, the contract terms concerning termination come into play. Termination provisions spell out in advance the rights of either party to halt the work and the compensation to be paid as a result. This particular contract specified that termination would result in the payment of all fees incurred up to that date.

However, the new executive refused to approve payment of the outstanding invoices. This dispute went all the way to formal arbitration before a settlement was reached.

This type of behavior is clearly not ethical, but occurs too frequently. Many years ago a major business newspaper featured an article about the difficulties independent consultants and others experience in getting paid by large companies. The article included a number of suggestions on how to reduce the risk (bill frequently, work on a retainer, insist on fifty percent up front), but the truly amazing part of the story was how frequently large companies failed to pay independent consultants.

There is only one excuse for hiring someone to do a job, then refusing to pay for it – you aren't satisfied with the work. That wasn't the case in any of the anecdotal situations presented in the article.

One problem for small companies is the cost and duration of the court process. A relatively small company is often faced with the business decision of challenging its adversary or accepting the loss. But this fact does not alter the unethical behavior of the larger entity.

The appropriate way for either party, regardless of relative size and strength, to modify the terms of an agreement is to sit down with the other party and openly discuss their issues with the existing agreement. Most contractors who want the business will listen to their client and attempt to be reasonable. Negotiation followed by a formal amendment to the contract, executed by both parties, is the only appropriate way to change the terms of a contract.

Other Types of Agreements

Not all business agreements are embodied in formal, written contracts. The time and expense involved in writing a formal contract may not be worth the consideration involved in the agreement. Even in these cases state law often provides protection to the parties.

For example, when you hire an electrician for home maintenance, he presents you with an estimate and you agree to let him do the work. If the work proves to be faulty, there are legal avenues for you to pursue even in the absence of a signed formal contract. On the electrician's side, he can get a Mechanics Lien on your house if you don't pay.

A common situation for engineering firms occurs when the prospective client must meet an urgent deadline or has an emergency situation. The client wants your company to start work as soon as possible, with the pledge to execute a contract based on the rates and services you have discussed.

In these situations, immediately draft a one or two page Letter of Agreement and ask the client to sign it. The Letter of Agreement provides a clear statement of what you are being hired to do and how much you will be paid. It can also document the intent to enter into a formal contract by a certain date. The Letter of Agreement provides protection for your firm, establishing that the client authorized your work and agreed to pay a certain amount.

Not paying for a service rendered is not ethical behavior. The lack of a formal contract does not remove the obligation to pay, nor does it remove either party from the legal process. Small claims courts and civil suits are available as remedies in most of the fifty states.

Beyond Payment

Contracts and agreements have many aspects other than documenting the service to be performed and the payment to be received. Other contract provisions may address matters such as:

- Duration of the agreement
- Publicity
- Identification of the customer in marketing and advertising
- Additional phases of work
- Quality assurance mechanisms
- Hiring of the other party's personnel

The number of provisions is as rich as human imagination. If these provisions are not in writing, but you have made a solid commitment that the other party believes in, then you have an ethical obligation to adhere to them.

Failure to Adhere to an Agreement

As stated above, state laws govern contracts and agreements between businesses and other parties. A party who believes its agreement was not honored has rights in the courts to pursue compensation or other settlement.

Nonetheless, ethical business behavior involves obeying the law, adhering to contracts and honoring agreements.

What happens when a company routinely violates its contracts and agreements? Very often the following events occur over time:

- The company's business shrinks. When people have been injured unfairly the word generally leaks out within the industry. Customers, suppliers and subcontractors begin to avoid doing business with an unethical company.

- The company's cost of business increases. Other parties will seek more favorable terms to decrease their risk of doing business with an organization whose track record is questionable.

- The quality of business the company receives decreases. The most reputable players will look elsewhere for the services or products the company provides.

- The quality of personnel the company attracts decreases. Good, trustworthy employees with experience will look elsewhere to work as their discomfort with the company's actions increases.

Mistakes

What is the professional and ethical way to handle situations in which one party violates a contract by mistake?

As discussed, formal contracts can be complex and lengthy, with many details. Just as the first step in obeying the law is to know the law, the first step in adhering to contracts is to know the contract and its provisions. An ethical organization will place someone in charge of contract compliance. That person is responsible for monitoring the project team's activity and ensures that her company's personnel follow the agreement.

In a smaller organization, the project director could be responsible for this function with some oversight from an executive. In modest size organizations, the internal counsel's office may share in this responsibility. The largest organizations often have a group of people who have the title "Contract Officers," "Program Officers," or something similar. Their mission is to keep the company in compliance with its agreements.

In spite of all best efforts, mistakes will still happen. When an ethical organization recognizes that it strayed from the contract, it will undertake the initiative to reconcile with the other party by following these steps.

1. Get the facts
2. Notify the other party
3. Recommend and negotiate a solution
4. Take steps to correct the problem
5. Take steps to prevent reoccurrence
6. If necessary, amend the contract

Get the facts. Make sure you know exactly what happened, how it happened, who was responsible and what the impact is on the activity covered by the agreement. Without the facts, you will be poorly prepared to resolve the matter and prevent its reoccurrence.

Notify the other party. This should be done promptly. While it is best to have the facts at hand first, if it will take more than a day to determine the facts, the other party should be at least notified that you have become aware of the matter and that you have launched an investigation. Check the contract itself. Many contracts, particularly those involving government agencies, will be very specific on the notification process, including how quickly the other party should be notified and who specifically within their organization should receive the notification. The contract may even specify what types of information you should provide and stipulate a formal written notice.

Recommend and negotiate a solution. The contract may specify how this is to be worked out. If it doesn't, you should take the steps to propose a recommendation to the other party. They should have an opportunity for input or to provide their own recommendation. Then work out a mutually satisfactory solution to the problem.

Take steps to correct the problem. With an agreement as to the solution, begin enacting the solution immediately, unless your negotiation provides for a schedule of repair. The right thing to do is to fix your failure as soon as possible.

Take steps to prevent reoccurrence. Part of the fact gathering should be focused on how the problem occurred so that corrective measures can be taken. You don't want to be in the position of having the same problem occur a second time. That reflects poorly on your company's competence, diligence and responsibility.

If necessary, amend the contract. As part of the determination of a solution, it sometimes becomes clear that the contract itself is partly at fault. It didn't specify something that it should have or it did specify something that needs to be changed. If that is the case, amending the contract should be a part of your recommended solution.

The above process will have a number of benefits for you:

- Your employees will recognize that you take both the quality of your work and the adherence to your agreements seriously. They will be more vigilant and have higher morale.

- Your internal processes for product manufacture and/or service delivery will always become more effective and efficient as a result of finding and correcting errors. A large body of Quality Assurance literature is devoted to the notion of finding errors before they occur and the benefits thereof. By taking steps to prevent future occurrence of contract violations, you will be taking advantage of this concept.

- Your suppliers, customers and alliance partners will quickly come to recognize that you are reliable, trustworthy and dependable. By owning up to your mistakes and correcting them quickly you will build constructive relationships that expand future business opportunities.

Chapter Four – The Third Layer: Professional Codes of Ethics

One of the most important layers in our business ethics model, The Seven Layers of Integrity®, is Professional Codes of Ethics. Most professions have a code of ethics that sets minimum standards of ethical behavior for license holders in that profession. Examples of professions include doctors, lawyers, engineers and accountants as well as architects, teachers and nurses.

Two important legal concepts apply to professionals and differentiate them from other occupations: fiduciary and agency.

Fiduciary Relationships and Agents

Fiduciary

Most readers of this book will have heard the term *fiduciary*. A fiduciary is a person (or entity) who has been entrusted to make decisions and conduct activity on behalf of and in the interests of another person or entity. For example, a person who is the trustee of a trust or the guardian over the assets of a minor child is a fiduciary.

While a fiduciary responsibility is usually related to the direct management of financial affairs, the concept of a *fiduciary relationship* can extend beyond the direct involvement with financial assets. For example, the Board of Directors and the Officers of a corporation have a fiduciary role with respect to that company and the interests of its shareholders, even though they may not make detailed decisions concerning specific financial transactions. Boards may have direct approval over a few financial decisions, such as issuing more shares or increasing quarterly dividends, but they are not normally involved in day-to-day operational decisions concerning the investment or expenditure of funds. Nonetheless, they have a fiduciary role.

Agent

The legal concept of *agency* actually is more general than that of fiduciary and applies to more situations. Indeed, the concept of agency is related to the concepts of organizations that evolved over the last several centuries and applies to anyone who is an employee, manager, or executive of a corporation. It also applies to any person or entity retained by a corporation to perform a service.

Agency involves two parties: the agent and the principal. The agent acts on behalf of the principal and is regarded as an instrument of the principal. The principal receives the benefits derived from the actions of its agents. For example, an employee is an agent and the employer is the principal.

The agent and principal relationship derives from the activity and the benefit for the principal; it does not derive from any benefit for the agent. This means that a person or entity can be an agent, under the law, even though they receive no payment or other benefit of any kind. For example, if you are an unpaid volunteer working for the Parent Teachers Association, you are an agent of the PTA.

In contemporary society, all of us are agents for many different kinds of organizations, associations and individuals. Many of us are also principals for others. For example, if you hire an electrician or an attorney or a housekeeper, then you are a principal and they are your agent.

The concepts of agent and fiduciary together with their associated responsibilities are highly relevant to the ethical standards found in the codes of ethics for professionals.

The Professions

Armed with some background on agents and fiduciaries, let us now focus attention on the professions, their characteristics and their codes of ethics.

Why are certain groups called professions and what sets them apart from other occupations?

Professions are occupations that have the following characteristics:

1. They require special training, usually at a college level

2. The individuals carry a designation that indicates they are part of the profession

3. They have a governing body that certifies the training, skills and fitness for practice of anyone holding the designation

4. They are generally self-regulating

5. They have processes in place for granting and withholding licenses that allow the individuals to state that they are certified and fit for practice

6. They have a code of ethics

7. As professionals, they have some discretion in making decisions in their work and in the organization

Consider CPAs as an example.

Special training in accounting and auditing is required to be a CPA.

The profession uses a designation (Certified Public Accountant or CPA) to indicate the individuals who are in the profession.

Each of the fifty states has a State Board of Public Accountancy or similarly titled organization that determines the specific training, skills and fitness for practice required for those holding the designation CPA. Candidates for CPA must, among other things, pass a very comprehensive written exam as part of receiving the right to use this designation.

The profession has been self-regulating (a recent hot topic of political discussion) and has done so via the State Boards and a national entity named the American Institute of Certified Public Accountants, or AICPA. (The Sarbanes-Oxley Act of 2002 altered the regulatory landscape, but only for CPAs who wish to practice before the Securities and Exchange Commission; auditors of publicly held companies are affected by this legislation but not your personal accountant who prepares your tax return.)

There are processes in place, resting with the fifty State Boards, for granting and withholding licenses, monitoring the compliance of the licensees with the rules of the profession and, if necessary, reprimanding individuals and firms for various types of rule infringement and unprofessional behavior. Included is the prospect of losing one's license either permanently or temporarily. (The Sarbanes-Oxley Act has also established the Public Company Accounting Oversight Board and empowered it to impose disciplinary actions with respect to accounting firms that wish to practice before the SEC.)

The profession has a code of ethics, promulgated by the State Boards.

CPAs have discretion in the decisions they make regarding the work products they produce.

Professions and the Law

Many of the professions are directly and indirectly under the jurisdiction of law. Typically, state government enacts a law that establishes a governing body of the profession. The law will provide that governing body with the authority to regulate the profession and its members. Most significant with respect to this authority is the right to determine who is able to publicly designate himself as a member of the profession. This is usually done via the issuance of a license to practice, which can be granted, withheld and removed by the governing body. People who have not been issued a license by the governing body are not legally allowed to designate themselves members of the profession.

Thus when a member of the general public seeks out a doctor or attorney, the existence of a license to practice medicine or law in that state tells the prospective buyer of services that the individual has been certified by the state through the governing body of the profession and is permitted by law to practice his or her profession in that state. The license in essence gives the public the assurance that the person has bona fide credentials – education, training, experience and the passing of examinations – necessary to practice medicine or law.

Within the accounting profession, the State Boards of Public Accountancy are the governing bodies responsible for carrying out the regulation of the profession. As with similar boards of physicians and attorneys, a State Board of Public Accountancy is usually comprised of accounting professionals, not politicians and regulators. That is why the profession has been said to be self-regulating. While the Sarbanes-Oxley Act alters that self-regulation, the majority of CPAs, who either work in industry or for firms that do not audit publicly held companies, continue to work in a primarily self-regulated environment.

Characteristics of Professional Codes of Ethics

A particular characteristic of the professions that is of interest to us in this book is the following: the governing body that grants and withholds the right to use its professional designation has usually promulgated a code of ethics for the profession.

In essence this means that if you are a Certified Public Accountant there is a group of people independent of your company, industry, civic community, friends and family and religion who have a voice in judging your behavior as ethical or not. The same is true for many other professions.

The judgment of these professional groups is focused on how you conduct yourself in carrying out both your work as a professional and your business as a professional.

The codes of ethics of the professions usually contain terms such as *due diligence* and *due care* related to the work you perform for your employer and the public. These requirements are used to ensure that the work performed has the highest possible quality and is in conformance with a set of standards for the profession.

Professional codes of ethics often include phrases such as "conflict of interest" and "independence and objectivity" that apply to the professional's conduct in relation to his employer and the public. The purpose of such provisions is to require the highest possible objectivity from the professional so that the professional's opinions and advice can be taken as seriously as possible. Hence the phrase "professional opinion."

The codes of ethics of the professions also incorporate the concepts of agency and fiduciary reviewed at the beginning of this chapter. Some professions, including accounting and law, are particularly focused on the issues regarding conflicts of interest and independence and objectivity. These issues are very relevant to attorneys and CPAs who undertake to represent their clients, act as their agents and, in many cases, have fiduciary elements in that representation.

Engineers may also face conflicts of interest, especially when signing off on the competence of products and processes. Engineers, in their technical roles, may feel pressured by management to sign off on safety standards when they may feel uncertain. One well-known example of this conflict is documented in the reports on the Challenger and the decision to launch despite the unusually cold temperatures. After Thiokol engineers recommended delaying the launch, a senior Thiokol manager asked the Vice President for Engineering to "take off his engineering hat and put on his management hat." The VP reversed his previous recommendation not to launch. In doing so, he took the view that the data was inconclusive despite the recommendations of his engineers. (1)

Characteristics of Professional Behavior

There are many definitions of what constitutes professional behavior, but in this book we focus in particular on those qualities that are closely related to ethical behavior.

In particular, ethical professional behavior:

1. Strives to use and apply the most accurate and up to date knowledge available to conduct the work involved
2. Welcomes assistance
3. Is open to scrutiny
4. Maintains objectivity
5. Maintains independence, providing full disclosure with respect to any conflicts – real, perceived or potential

6. Actively challenges anything that it believes is wrong

Let's examine each of these in detail.

Applies the most current knowledge. A professional is obligated to use due diligence and due care. An important aspect of due care is actively seeking to be fully aware of the most recent advances in your field and apply the most current knowledge and techniques. Many fields, such as engineering, architecture and medicine, are subject to continual scientific advancement. In other fields, such as accounting and law, there are continual changes in the field itself as new regulations are passed, the tax code changes and the law evolves.

A professional is not sloppy. She does not develop something in a rushed setting with numerous interruptions and then present it as a final product. She will double check her work and make sure it is right. That is part of due diligence and due care.

To maintain currency, most professions have on-going education requirements. If the professional is not attending conferences or receiving other sources of training, then recent developments will pass him by and his professional competence can come into question. Engineers, CPAs and attorneys have Continuing Professional Education requirements that must be met each year to maintain their license.

Welcomes assistance. A professional who is fully engaged in the notion of due care will actively seek advice and assistance when he is uncertain of his own expertise. All of the professions are engaged in complex activities and it is impossible for a single person to be expert in all aspects of the profession's field of knowledge. A professional will take no shame in seeking the advice and review of others in his field. Providing the best service to the employer or client, who is the principal, is paramount.

Is open to scrutiny. Professionals should always be open and above board about their work and their business relationships. Most professions require their licensees to cooperate fully with any investigation. Professionals who have done their best work, who have applied the most current expertise and sought the advice of other experts, should not hesitate to have their work reviewed. If an honest mistake is found, the professional will take steps to immediately correct it and learn from it. A professional does not become defensive, attempt to hide a mistake or become emotional about defending himself. A professional would welcome scrutiny in the same manner and for the same reasons as welcoming assistance and trying to learn the most she possibly can about her field.

Similarly, professionals should be open to scrutiny involving their business relationships and potential conflicts of interest. These issues are important to the general public, employers and customers. Professionals will conduct their affairs in a way that is honest and open. They are aware of conflict of interest issues and will take steps to ensure that such potential conflicts are exposed and resolved, even if it means the loss of a financial or other opportunity.

Maintains objectivity. Professionals are objective. That means they can look at their own activities and work in an objective manner, as if it were the work of a colleague in their field. When called upon to make a decision regarding an issue about the work, they exclude friendships, desires for advancement, personal vacation plans and business relationships in reaching that decision.

A professional engineer, recognizing that a significant flaw exists in a bridge design, should not let the prospect of a resulting fee overrun preclude him from doing what is right and correcting the flaw. A professional attorney, faced with a change in court date for his client, will work the weekend to make sure his client's case is ready even though he had other personal plans. A professional accountant, called upon to audit a key area of a client company, will be forthright with his firm about his lack of experience in that area even though the assignment could lead to a faster promotion.

Maintains independence, providing full disclosure. Professionals must be independent of their clients or customers. That means that there are no relationships with the client or customer that would place pressure on the professional to cut corners or be less than fully candid about an important issue. It also means there are no relationships with a client's competitors or others in the business community that would place the professional in a position of conflict of interest.

A familiar example of a potential conflict of interest is the situation in which an audit firm has substantial non-audit revenue coming from an audit client. The accounting profession's codes of ethics are very clear about the need for auditors to maintain their independence and objectivity. Having significant non-audit revenue from the client makes it difficult to maintain independence when the audit detects a problem that the client does not want to resolve or disclose.

Engineers can face a conflict of interest if they are receiving compensation from a client and subsequently asked to present a public report on that same company's compliance with regulation. In these situations, the engineer must disclose the full nature of his relationship with the company as part of his public report.

Attorneys always review their client list before taking on a new client; they must determine that the new client does not present a potential conflict of interest with an existing client relationship.

<u>Actively challenges identified wrongs.</u> This is perhaps the hardest part of all professional behavior, because it calls on the professional to initiate potential conflict with others. Whistle blowing and its consequences are topics beyond the scope of this book, but they originate with this premise: when a professional sees something that is an error, he or she must bring attention to it.

An excellent example of this situation is the problem with the O-Rings that led to the Challenger disaster. In this case, an engineer recognized the potential for O-Ring failure under the particular temperature changes and conditions experienced by the shuttle overnight. The individual brought the matter to the attention of his superiors, but along the way a very valid concern was overlooked or discounted in the decision to go ahead with the launch. The engineer did the right thing – he actively pursued the matter. Management, or at least the complex management decision process that led to a launch, failed.

Another familiar example is Sherron Watkins at Enron, who challenged the accounting treatment of the off-the-book partnerships created by the CFO, Andrew Fastow. She took the matter to Ken Lay, Chairman of the Board, in a famous letter that was later published in *The New York Times*. She also called the accounting firm, Arthur Andersen & Co., and raised the issue with them. Ms. Watkins is an accounting professional and was a licensed CPA at the time she took these actions.

In these high profile situations, the individual takes on the challenge recognizing that his or her job, if not a career, is potentially at risk. The stakes can be very high in these cases and result in a situation in which the individual may have great difficulty being hired by someone else.

However, many situations are simply a matter of routine day-to-day business. A programmer identifies a design error and brings it to management's attention. Management is grateful and fixes the design. An architect recognizes that a particular material is not going to have the strength needed to support a key truss in the building. She brings it to attention, and the material selection is changed or the design of the support structure is modified. This is part of being a professional. It is an active challenge of imperfection, part of the goal of bringing the very best quality and competence to one's work.

Conflicts for Professionals

In the current business environment, there are many opportunities for conflict between employees who strive to be professionals and their employers or others. These conflicts can often be resolved openly and constructively. It is, of course, the extreme cases that get publicity. The thousands of other situations are never mentioned in the public press because they are not visible; their constructive resolution contributes to that invisibility.

Perhaps the single most important person a professional will have conflicts with is himself.

Surprised? You shouldn't be. Consider four of our six professional qualities:

- Welcomes assistance
- Is open to scrutiny
- Maintains objectivity
- Maintains independence

How many of us, no matter how well intentioned, can continually be at our very best with respect to these characteristics? It is difficult to set ego aside and admit that we don't know everything. It is hard to have others, who may have hidden agendas of their own, scrutinize your work without becoming defensive. Can you be truly objective about the value of what you have done? Can you admit a mistake you have found, knowing its potential impact on your career or upcoming promotion? Can you sacrifice that one chance at a great investment because you realize you need to have full disclosure of potential conflicts of interest?

Depending on your personality, you may have trouble with one or more of these qualities. You should take time to sit down with yourself and identify your weak spots. Then begin a process of self-education. If you have difficulty working with others (don't welcome assistance, not open to scrutiny), now would be a good time to examine why that is the case and reset your thinking and outlook. Teamwork is an important quality that employers look for in today's world. Improving your teamwork skills would be a good thing for many reasons.

If you have trouble being objective when you need to be, try to determine the reasons and resolve to be alert to situations where greater objectivity is needed so you can respond to them more professionally. If you face a potential conflict of interest situation, sit down with yourself and your spouse and examine it; then determine how to bring it up and get it resolved. Most employers will not fault you for bringing a matter to their attention if it keeps them out of potential trouble. If you have to pass on an opportunity, be clear about the reasons. Others will generally think well of you if you explain the conflict to them and why it is not good professional ethics for you to be involved at this time.

Some of the more common conflicts that professionals experience in their work include:

Acceptance of sloppy work

No one says that they accept sloppy work. But a lot of sloppy work gets done all the same. Some of the more obvious reasons include: lack of necessary skills to do the job well; unrealistic deadlines; inept supervision and/or management; and company culture.

At a minimum, you should work hard to make certain that your own contribution is your best effort, has been double-checked for accuracy and completeness and that you are noting your mistakes and learning from them. If you are a supervisor, don't get in the habit of cleaning up the work of your team because "it's faster that way" or "they won't get it done right."

The only way for people to know that sloppy work is unacceptable is for them to have to do it over. Be sure to communicate precisely what is wrong and what your standards are. Take the role of a teacher and regard this as an investment of your time today so that your team will be working more efficiently next week and next month.

Difficulty in staying current

All companies are trying to do more work with fewer people. All of us are faced with endless meetings that consume time we could have used to get our work done. Deadlines are tight and competition is fierce. So it is no surprise that staying technically current in your field can be a challenge. The professional literature stacks up, the desired training is rescheduled, and hands on opportunities to learn new skills are not available.

Look for new ways to maintain currency with greater efficiency. If there is an area you want to know more about, find a couple of people who have experience and take them to lunch. Pick their brains and find out what's going on. Ask what the hot issues are and find out how they stay current in this area. Two such lunches per month will be a good investment and not really take additional time out of your day.

If the professional literature is stacking up, take a lunch hour to glance through the tables of contents. Pick out one article from each and make it a point to read that one. If you fly on business, always take some current literature with you. Or if there are other times that are often dead times, such as waiting on customer appointments, have one of those journals available. Automobile and train commutes are good times to listen to an audio book that you've wanted to read.

Lack of support for continuing education

While many companies are willing to help you in meeting the continuing education requirements necessary to maintain your professional license or certification, some are not. You may have trouble getting the time, let alone financial support, necessary to complete those hours.

Look to your direct supervisor and human resources department for assistance. Make them aware of the issue and its importance to you (and others in your company who have similar requirements). Be willing to work with them and be flexible. If it appears that your company cannot support this effort, resolve to make the sacrifices necessary or look for an employer who can.

Other Conflicts

Examples of other potential conflicts are:

Resistance to involving necessary experts

Management is cost conscious. The need for additional expertise of the right kind is often resisted on that basis. When a professional identifies that additional expertise is needed, but management resists the costs, conflict will result. Depending upon the relative importance of the need for this expertise and the significance of the overall work product being produced, this conflict could become a very serious one for the professional and the company.

Encountering hidden agendas

There is nothing more stifling of open scrutiny and general honesty than the hidden agendas of individuals in the company that would impair the openness required. Moreover, there are often times when the political agendas of individuals and groups within a company are detrimental to professional objectivity, work against the application of the best possible expertise and impair professional independence.

Exposing perceived wrongs

The most serious conflict for a professional is one in which a company is clearly embarked on a course of action that violates the law. A host of legal and personal issues come in to play and the stakes can become very high. This situation can be a true challenge to any professional faced with the choice of keeping silent or becoming a whistle blower.

Summary

Professions, professional standards and professional codes of ethics apply directly to specific endeavors. But the principles behind these standards and codes are grounded in the law (via the legal concepts of agency and fiduciary) and serve as a sound basis for behavior in any business or occupation. While many readers may not be members of a specific profession, all of us would benefit from adopting the concepts of professional behavior to our business and personal endeavors.

Indeed, when thinking about a business action or activity, the very next question that should be asked (after "Is it legal?" and "Does it violate a contract or agreement?") should be "Is it professional?"

Footnotes

(1) *Columbia Accident Investigation Board (CAIB) Report 2003,* page 100, as discussed in Phillip K. Tompkins' *Apollo, Challenger, Columbia: The Decline of the Space Program,* Roxbury Publishing, 2005, page 115.

Chapter Five – The Fourth Layer: Industry Standards

Every company, organization or group of people operates in the context of what can be called a *business environment*. The business environment surrounds and is composed of the standard ways in which business is commonly conducted across all companies or organizations of like kind in the same industry.

For example, companies in the real estate development industry have common ways of conducting business and running day-to-day operations – choosing raw land for suburban tracts, contracting with construction firms, working with local and state government agencies, and closing a sale.

The same is true in every industry group. There is a normal way of operating, or doing business, that can be found in most or all of the companies in that industry. The same can be said of non-profit organizations, charities, churches, high school administrations and academia.

Accepted Industry Practices

In examining ethical business behavior, we must consider the perspective of the business environment – the cross-company norms and accepted practices that apply to that industry. This is not to say that a particular industry's standards are ethical or even legal. The industry standard simply provides another perspective that can be applied in analyzing a decision or behavior. This perspective recognizes the standards and accepted practices within the industry and business environment.

For example, the insurance industry often awards commissioned sales agents for *production* – the generation of new business. At one time, most insurance companies set production goals, created sales clubs and rewarded agents when they met certain production criteria. One of those rewards for the top producers, agents who had generated the highest levels of new sales of life insurance products during the prior twelve months, was an all-expenses-paid bonus vacation in Hawaii.

Where did the money come from to pay for these trips? It came from the profits taken from the company before taxes, stockholders' dividends and earnings. In other words, shareholders received smaller dividends and had less stock appreciation because of these trips. Was that fair or ethical?

In the eyes of the government it was legal. The tax code allows companies to deduct such expenses, provided they are usual and customary. In other words, such expenses can be deducted if they are in line with those of other companies in the same business or industry. Since all the insurance companies had these or similar bonus plans for agents, one company's shares of stock were not unduly penalized versus similar investments. As to the earnings and dividends, one can always balance the incremental cost of the bonus with the higher motivation and sales generation of both the agents who received the bonus and the many others who strived toward that goal.

In short, this type of reward, in the context of the business/industry environment, was a standard accepted practice.

Saying that ethical industry behavior is established by common practice may sound similar to saying that behavior is ethical if everyone else is doing it. But we are only judging the behavior from one ethical perspective: the perspective of that industry's standards. Judging the behavior from the other perspectives or layers in our model may result in a different conclusion.

Characteristics of Industry Standards

Most industry standards arise over an extended period of time and as a result of collective experience about what works and what doesn't. They evolve based on interaction between parties in the industry and between those parties and their customers, suppliers, bankers, and others. The approaches that seem to work best become established as the standard way of doing business. They serve an important role as an unwritten short hand on acceptable behavior and provide a common standard of operation, making the industry more efficient. Eventually, people in the industry often forget the history of other methods that failed and the industry standards become established and accepted.

An industry's standards and ways of doing business consist of rules that are generally unwritten, although some of them may have evolved into local, state or even federal law. If the industry is heavily based on a particular profession (such as engineers, physicians, psychologists and accountants) then that profession's code of ethics or other body of standards will often have documented the industry standards. But generally, many industry standards are undocumented.

Individual employees and business people usually acquire an understanding of the industry standards through training and experience. When you work in the industry long enough, you come to understand how the game is played.

The hotel industry provides another example.

Every hotel chain in America has a room reservation system and a price tag for staying in a room. Those prices vary by hotel location, room size, number and size of beds, amenities, and floor location. They can be discounted substantially if you are with a convention or other large group. If you belong to the AAA (American Automobile Association) or AARP (American Association of Retired Persons), you may be eligible for a discount. If you are not associated with a group and you make a reservation, you are very likely to be quoted the *rack* rate. The rack rate is the industry term for the standard, undiscounted, rate for a particular type of room. It is generally higher than most people ever pay for a room. As a result, when you book a reservation, the price you get is very likely to vary from what someone else pays. Is that ethical?

Probably the only way to answer that question, apart from whether or not it breaks the law, is to recognize that this is a common business practice across the hotel industry. If the discounts were based on the ethnic background or religion of the party staying at the facility that would be clearly illegal and unethical. But when the variation is based on factors that are clearly business related, it is another matter. If one person stays in a room with two double beds and another person stays in a suite with a king size bed and kitchenette, the difference in pricing is accepted.

Conventions and members of a large group commonly receive discounted hotel prices.

Changing Industry Standards

When people violate an industry standard, there are only three things that can happen: (1) nothing; (2) they can be perceived as innovators; and (3) they can be perceived as disreputable.

Nothing generally happens if the impact on the industry itself is minimal. If a given hotel has a policy of not providing discounts to members of the AAA, nothing is likely to happen to that hotel.

But when the change is significant, then care should be taken on how it is enacted.

Many years ago, before Enron's financial crisis began, the company's leadership decided to significantly decrease its reliance on regulated industry, such as gas pipeline companies and natural gas pipeline transmission. Management recognized that unregulated industry segments were more profitable and decided to position more of their operations in that arena. At the same time, Enron began trying to create new markets in products such as electricity and fiber optic bandwidth. Their idea was that electricity and bandwidth could be treated as commodities, similar to oil and natural gas. By "commoditizing" these products and creating a market for them, Enron could change the face of the power and communication industries.

At the time, many viewed this as extremely innovative. Enron became an industry leader, a company that presented a strategy to be imitated. Companies that jumped on the bandwagon included Williams, Dynegy, Reliant and many others. Enron during the 1990s had a reputation as the place to be, the ones out in front, the company to scramble to keep up with. They were perceived as competitors and innovators in a positive sense. They were expanding their industry thereby creating potential opportunity for others.

By contrast, and during the same period, Microsoft was facing legal problems and intense criticism in its own industry – computer software products. Why was that? Microsoft was innovative. Microsoft was a leader.

Certainly some of the criticism Microsoft received may have been a result of jealousy or a desire to slow down the juggernaut with legal action. But a great deal of the criticism, in our opinion, was based on how Microsoft was perceived in its ways of doing business within its own industry.

Microsoft was perceived as acting in a way that did not increase the vitality of its industry but rather made it more difficult for others in the industry to compete. Microsoft was accused of using its marketing strength and size to create deals with hardware manufacturers that would make it more difficult for competitors to have a fair opportunity to sell their products. Microsoft allegedly deliberately withheld information about how its products functioned so that competitors would have difficulty integrating with Microsoft products. Microsoft allegedly attempted to "own" the desktop, meaning that when a PC is booted up, the only icons that would appear on the desktop would initially be those of Microsoft products. Users would have to take additional steps to load icons of competing products onto their desktop.

In short, Microsoft's alleged actions were perceived as stifling competition.

Over a period of years, major players in the software industry challenged Microsoft, first publicly in the press, then by attracting the attention of the government's anti-trust machinery. Bill Gates, the founder and chairman of Microsoft, was forced to testify. In the end a settlement was reached.

What did Microsoft do that the later more vilified Enron did not? Microsoft acted in a way that its competitors in its own industry perceived to be unfair and an impediment to competition. By contrast, Enron was perceived in its industry as having created new opportunities for all.

Being an innovator is often a matter of how a company portrays itself – if you want to break the rules of your industry it is best to do so in a way that creates new opportunity for the industry as a whole. Break the rules in other ways and you may create enemies instead of admiration.

From an industry perspective, ethical behavior is simply behavior that conforms to the existing standards of the industry or stretches the standards in a way that is fair to others and increases opportunity for all.

It should be assumed that existing standards and new initiatives are within the bounds of law and don't violate existing contracts and agreements. Enron was later disgraced as it became clear that part of its strategy was to employ financial techniques of questionable legality.

Industry Standards and Individual Behavior

By using industry standards as one perspective for judging behavior, we accept the collective experience of an industry as something valuable and worth consideration. By also looking at the behavior from the other perspectives explored in this book, we avoid using them without question and hope to find the places where they break down.

An important perspective for employees of all kinds, from janitorial staff and security guards to top executives, involves the concept of agency introduced in the last chapter. Companies do not act; people do. Every inappropriate action, unethical action and illegal action is made by one or more people acting in the role of agent on the company's behalf. We should always remember that our actions reflect on the organization as well as ourselves. We have a responsibility to the company, its shareholders, its customers and business partners to act as best we can.

If, as agents, we also have a fiduciary role with respect to the company, then a higher standard is certainly implied. Whether as purchasing agents, accountants, managers and executives or CFO and CEO, our fiduciary responsibility is to make the best possible use of the company's financial assets for the good of the company.

As a part of their role as agents, employees should make it a point to know, understand and make use of the best practices in the industry, including the best practices regarding ethical behavior and adherence to accepted industry standards.

Industry Behavior and the Law

What happens when industry norms violate the law or appear to be unethical from the perspective of one of the other layers in our model?

In the role of agent and possibly fiduciary, we should make certain that adherence to the law is the first priority. It is irresponsible to choose another course. In another chapter we will further explore the potential conflict between a corporate culture or industry environment and the responsibility of individuals, as agents, fiduciaries or professionals, to adhere to the law and to raise issues of illegality to management.

For the purpose of illustrating that conflict, we need look no further than the recent difficulties of the investment banking industry.

For years, investment bankers had tremendous influence over the operations of their firms. Major players such as Salomon Smith Barney, Goldman Sachs and others had a combination of investment bankers and financial analysts. The investment bankers put deals together for companies. Such deals include the initial public offering (IPO) of a young company's stock, subsequent rounds of capital acquisition through the public markets, mergers with other companies and acquisitions of others. For this work, the investment bankers earned very large sums of money and therefore held the political power within their organizations.

By contrast, the financial analysts of the same firms provided services that garnered smaller revenues. Their job was to analyze the financial statements, operations, market positioning and potential future revenue and earnings of publicly traded companies and develop reports to investors advising them to buy, sell or hold shares of the company.

The potential for conflict between these two groups within the same investment banking firm were enormous. If a financial analyst recommended that investors hold or sell the stock of a particular company while the investment bankers were trying to get business from that same company, then the financial analysts were jeopardizing the much larger revenue stream generated by the investment bankers.

In theory, the firms maintained a "Chinese wall" between the two groups and postured in public that these internal barriers kept the financial analysts' recommendations independent. But as the facts have come out, that was not nearly the case.

In a number of firms, the outright disagreement between analysts and investment bankers on the prospects of a company's stock were captured in e-mails and other documents that surfaced after government investigations were launched. And the investment bankers always won. So while the analysts were thinking that a company's IPO shares were worth $3, the firm was still telling its customers to buy the $15 stock.

The power and influence of the investment bankers was such that they could end the career of a financial analyst who got in their crosshairs. And, as has become clear, this was the normal practice in the industry, regardless of internal policies and statements by their CEOs.

In 2002, the Attorney General for the State of New York began investigating these practices at Merrill Lynch, Salomon Smith Barney and others. As documents came to light, the public became more and more displeased. Shortly after, Sanford Weill, the CEO of Citigroup, replaced the head of Citigroup's Salomon Smith Barney subsidiary and announced: "Although we have found nothing illegal, looking back, we can see that certain of our activities do not reflect the way we believe business should be done." (1)

What he acknowledged was that the industry standards, as carried out at Salomon Smith Barney, were now an embarrassment to the company.

The lesson is this: when industry standards either violate the law or violate the broader community's sense of fair play, they will eventually be exposed to the embarrassment of all and perhaps the intense legal difficulty of a few.

Summary

Industry standards provide an important perspective to apply in examining business decisions from an ethical perspective. However, the violation of industry standards is not always ethically wrong nor is the adherence to those standards necessarily right. This perspective therefore cannot be used in isolation.

Industry standards usually do not originate with the objective of conflicting with the law. When industry standards do violate the law or come into conflict with new legislation, government and others will eventually respond through lawsuits and indictments.

Footnotes

(1) *Citigroup Press Release,* September 8, 2002.

Chapter Six – The Fifth Layer:
Social, Civic and Geographic Communities

Beyond the law, contracts, industry standards and professional codes of ethics lies the greater community in which we live and work.

That greater community is really composed of many different communities: geographic, social, political and others. Each of these communities has its set of standards as well, and judgments concerning what constitutes ethical behavior will vary among them. The perspective each brings to ethical business dealings will vary. In general, those perspectives are more demanding – that is, they expect more from corporations and business people than the law, the industry and even the professions. At the same time, they are more nebulous – imprecise and subject to the group's revision based on the current crisis.

There are exceptions, of course, particularly in certain ethnic and immigrant population subcultures in which views of ethical business behavior are based on the customs of different countries and civilizations, sometimes at a level that differs from the U.S. standards. We will not take up these issues in this book, but rather continue to focus on ingrained U.S. standards.

Types of Communities and Classifications

Within the greater community exists a plethora of specific communities, or groups of people who have opinions and perspectives on behavior. By a *community*, we mean a group of people who have a shared interest. People within these groups may very well not know each other on an individual basis.

For example, the "investing public" could be regarded as such a community. People in this group come from all walks of life across our nation and most of them do not know each other. Yet they have some shared interests when it comes to the questions of what constitutes ethical business behavior. Equally important, from a business view, is the fact that their perspectives, when suitably organized or activated, can bring powerful political and social forces together to impact existing standards of behavior.

In this book, we want to restrict the identification and discussion of these communities to those that have relevant perspectives on ethical business behavior. In order to simplify the discussion, we have categorized them into four main groups: Political, Cultural, Social/Civic and Religious.

Political Communities

Political communities are groups of people whose shared interests are related to political territories and issues. These include geographic communities, political parties and organizations, and other groups with shared political interests.

Geographic Communities

Geographic communities are probably the easiest to identify in that they are tied to specific places on the map. The American people as a whole constitute such a community, as does each of the fifty states. Other geographic communities include counties, cities, school districts, congressional districts and neighborhoods.

With respect to business ethics, these geographic communities are rarely involved as communities that set standards for business behavior, with the exception of electing a body of representatives to enact and revise the laws that oversee business activity.

However, there are specific times when geographic communities do become involved in business behavior. Most typically this involvement will center on either jobs or the environment.

A recent example was the possible sale of Hershey Foods, the famous chocolate manufacturer located in Hershey, Pennsylvania. The prospect of the company being taken over by a foreign operation (Nestle) roused the local community to angry and concerned protest. While the prospect of lost jobs was a highly important item, citizen concern went beyond jobs to focus on an entire way of life and local culture. Citizens worried that acquisition by a company such as Nestle, based in Switzerland, would result in a deterioration of the community/company relationship that has existed for so long. In the end, the board of the Hershey Foundation, whose shares would have been sold, decided to not sell its shares and Hershey remains wedded to Hershey, Pennsylvania.

Ecological issues also can weigh heavily on geographic communities and have been a factor in many disputes between citizen groups and corporations.

In general, the ethical perspectives of geographic communities today are focused on two behavioral issues: sacrificing workers for the sake of profits and sacrificing the ecology for the sake of profits. The views of geographic communities often differ from those of shareholders and investors on these matters. Additionally, geographic communities call on corporations to consider the overall economic devastation of a community when job loss is at issue. This concern is especially true when a single company provides the majority of economic wealth to the local community.

In short, geographic communities hold businesses to a higher standard – one that weighs community impact, both economic and ecological, as an important factor in corporate decisions and recognizes that shareholders are not the only people impacted by corporate behavior and decisions.

Political Parties and Political Organizations

The major and minor political parties and other related organizations (for example, various Political Action Committees, the National Rifle Association, and the American Civil Liberties Union) are also relatively easy to identify in that they have specific members and formal organizations with a headquarters, spokespeople and pronouncements on what they stand for.

Although some readers may question the role either major party can play in the discussion of business ethics that would be missing the point. The point is that the members of these communities, who are generally voting citizens in control of potential monetary contributions, have an influence on the shape of legislation and selection of court judges and therefore have a long-term impact on the definition of ethical business behavior.

Political parties themselves tend to be motivated, in the area of business, by their constituencies. But there are times, such as we are now going through, when both parties sense the concerns of American voters and reshape their views of appropriate business behavior. Nonetheless, in the authors' opinions, these perspectives are a reflection of the concerns of other communities in the body politic.

Other political organizations run a broad range of perspectives. On the far right are those who favor a very laissez-faire approach to business, seek to limit government regulation and in essence build a case for leaving business alone, provided it obeys the law. On the far left are those who tend to perceive almost any business activity as suspicious at best.

Business professionals should be aware of the political forces they face in their particular industry and what their behavioral perceptions are. Forces once aroused are not easily called off, and the process of dealing with them can cost time, money and loss of good will among customers and the public. It is best to weigh the perception of political groups that may be opposed to one's actions and work with them, if possible, to reach acceptable solutions. Ignoring these groups will not make them go away and, in the event that their concerns turn out to have been justified, ignoring them will cast a pall on public perception of the company's ethics.

Vested Interest Communities

Vested interest communities are similar to other political organizations but lack the formal organization and structure of a Political Action Committee or similar organization. Vested interest communities do not have a membership roster or paying dues members. They may be unofficially represented by certain organizations, but not always. The significant characteristic of these communities is that their members have a shared interest in a particular type of political issue that involves a business or industry. Good examples of vested interest communities are the investing public, the health consumer, consumers, high tech workers, small business owners and blue-collar workers.

Within each of these groups is a common standard of expectations that has been set for a relevant industry or segment of business. Health consumers have expectations regarding the availability of access to medical facilities and the affordability of health care in general. They expect to have access to information about treatment options and the causes of disease. They often perceive health care providers as somehow colluding with drug companies and others to the detriment of the public.

These are important matters for the health care industries (healthcare providers, insurers and pharmaceutical companies). Public perception of behavior can lead to a number of challenges for the industry including changes in health care regulation and laws, economic alterations of the industry and restrictions on pricing. In addition, many health care consumers are no longer willing to take someone else's word for what constitutes the best treatment regimen or whether a new drug has been fully tested for adverse consequences. They are willing to challenge the industry individually and collectively.

Vested interest communities have expectations of ethical business behavior. These expectations consistently include the following:

Honesty

Simply defined, vested interest communities expect business people and companies to tell the truth at all times. Lying is not permitted. Close on the heels of lying is *spinning* – telling a story with a slant favorable to the company. This is generally seen as a sign that there is something the company is trying to hide. Spinning is deliberate and less than truthful; therefore it is perceived as deceptive.

Fair Play

Fair Play invokes the expectation that you will deal with me consistently with the rules that you told me about when I signed on the dotted line.

Health care consumers sometimes have a strong perception that HMOs do not engage in fair play.

Level Playing Field

Level Playing Field is the expectation that you will treat one member of the group with the same rules as other members of the group. There are no favorites. Everyone gets the same opportunities and the same restrictions.

The investing public is particularly upset about the offering of IPO shares to top executives to the exclusion of other, qualified investors and the recently disclosed after hours trading in mutual funds.

Do What is Right

Do What is Right is the expectation that, when it comes to actions with significant consequences, business will disregard profits in order to save lives, protect the general public and provide for its loyal employees. While *right* is the subject of this whole book and a concept that can never be fully explained, the public is often extremely accurate when it comes to judging individual situations.

When an HMO refuses to pay for the covered and necessary operation that will save your child's life, that is not perceived as "doing right." When company executives walk away with millions in severance packages while lifetime workers have their retirement benefits cut, that is not perceived as "doing right." When a financial analyst walks out the door with a multi-million dollar severance package and the investors who bought his recommended stocks have tremendous losses, that is not perceived as "doing right."

The concept of "Do What is Right" can, of course, conflict with the law and contracts. It may well be that the CEO and the financial analyst had well-written contracts that could not be broken. But the perception is that the analyst was unfairly rewarded for his poor work and the employees were unfairly treated compared to the CEO.

Most corporations would do well to think through the potential perception of the public before actions go astray. Politicians have a phrase that the corporate sector could take advantage of: "How will it play in Peoria?"

Cultural Communities

The United States is indeed the melting pot of the world's ethnic groups and cultures. We have a vast and rich array of cultural communities, many of which are filled with hard-working and enterprising people dedicated to making their lives better and living the American Dream.

As noted in the introduction to this chapter, it is beyond the scope of this book to attempt to portray the perceptions of ethical behavior that exist among these different communities. To the extent that these populations become assimilated, their views will eventually gravitate toward those of other Americans. Most cultural communities have expectations of ethical behavior that are similar to those outlined above for vested interest groups: honesty, fair play, a level playing field and "doing what is right." Of these, the level playing field may have more importance, if only in terms of discrimination issues. It should go without saying that companies and individuals in business should not discriminate on any basis.

Social/Civic Communities

Social and civic organizations also play a role in setting general community standards. These communities include public service organizations such as the Red Cross and the United Way as well as the Kiwanis, Rotary International, the Lions and others. Many formal social organizations have seen membership roles decrease as younger generations are not attracted to them and busy professionals don't have time to devote to them. The more public service focused organizations continue to remain strong, particularly those devoted to local community charity work.

These organizations do have expectations from the business community. They have an expectation that businesses will be run with integrity and contribute to the local community. That contribution should come in both dollars and time. A definite expectation is that upper management and executives will be personally involved. A Chairman of the Board of a major local organization is often placed in charge of development or fund raising for specific needs.

Would these organizations welcome someone whose ethical behavior is seen as undesirable? Clearly someone who has broken the law or caused many in the local community to lose money would not be welcome at most of these organizations. On the other hand, if potential ethical issues have been hidden from the public eye, then the name and prestige of the executive team can still be of value.

Our personal experience is that the influence of these organizations on the actual behavior of corporations is minimal.

Religious Communities

Religious organizations – the churches, synagogues and mosques of formal denominations – also set standards of behavior with respect to business ethics. It is rare for a religious organization, particularly a broader denomination, to take on the business community as a whole or a specific company with respect to ethical behavior. When they do, it is often in the context of a local community issue.

The overall expectations are not very different from those of social and civic organizations with a few key exceptions.

The exceptions are those areas that hit a hot button for a particular religious group. The most frequent current areas of conflict in behavior expectations deal with abortion, sex education and human genetic research and cloning. Corporations working in these areas may find that the ethical behavior issues involved have more to do with the fundamental business focus than the specific actions of individuals within the company.

In many ways, the conflicts between business and religious communities that are focused on the above issues are very similar to and tend to overlap those that arise with certain political action groups and vested interest communities (such as the Pro-Life movement).

Summary

The most significant and meaningful additional perspectives on ethical business behavior that arise out of the political and social communities are those related to how a company conducts itself with respect to the general public or local community. In the above classification, those issues arise with respect to geographic communities (cities) and vested interest communities (such as healthcare consumers). These communities call on business to focus on a higher moral territory – that of the role they play in people's lives, including, specifically, the lives of people who are not actual employees or business partners.

The Community Layer in The Seven Layers of Integrity® provides additional ethical standards beyond those found in the Law, Contracts, Professional Codes of Ethics and Industry Standards. Community standards can be relatively dormant for a long time but rapidly awaken when these groups believe that a wrong has occurred. Progressive corporations and businesses will do well to understand the needs and concerns of the broader public they serve and the local communities they operate in and then do their best to live up to these additional standards and expectations.

Chapter Seven – The Sixth Layer: Personal Relationships

Introduction

Two additional views of ethical business behavior arise from a more individual perspective – personal relationships and spiritual values.

Personal relationships, the subject of this chapter, clearly involve more than one person; yet they are closely associated with individuals as opposed to the kinds of groups, communities and organizations we have been discussing thus far.

Personal relationships – how we interact with others and our expectations of behavior in interpersonal relationships – have a tremendous influence on how we participate in the activities of business and how we perceive the behavior of businesses and business people.

How We Interact with Family and Friends

The common starting point for personal relationships is in the *family of origin* – the family we grew up in. Within the family we first learned how to interact with others and formed our earliest views of right and wrong. While Americans tend to have a very idealistic view of the family, family life can sometimes be rough stuff. The doting attention we may have experienced at the beginning can become less focused or even distant as we grow older. Our siblings compete for attention.

As we grow up, we learn the unspoken rules of the household, whatever those may be. For some, these are positive, constructive experiences. For others the family of origin was a very difficult place to be. For most of us, it was a mixture. But whatever the circumstances, there was a set of rules to be followed and we learned what they are.

What is interesting about families is that the rules are rarely discussed openly and never actually written down. Somehow we just learned that dinnertime was a time for fierce debate about every aspect of life or a time when Mom and Dad fought bitterly or a time when everyone politely focused on his or her meal and didn't talk. Somehow we learned that certain topics should never be brought up outside the immediate family. We learned our boundaries of openness and communication with others.

An additional part of growing up is learning to interact with others. We learned to play with others and probably experienced early disappointments with some of those interactions. Our childhood sweetheart wasn't interested. Our sister stole our first boyfriend. The kid down the street wrecked our brother's bicycle.

All of these experiences shaped how we relate and interact with people today and what we expect from others as a standard of behavior. And therein lies a problem for business, since a corporation's activities and actions are, at root, an ill structured composite of the actions and attitudes of the people that lead it and work in it.

Interpersonal Standards are Undocumented and Evolving

Just as the rules of our family of origin were undocumented and often unspoken, so are the rules we use in interacting with other people. Moreover, those rules evolve – grow, develop, change shape – as the relationships evolve and as we grow older. We expect more from our closest friends than we do from co-workers and more from our co-workers than from a casual business acquaintance. As adults, we have different standards than when we were teenagers and college students.

Our expectations of behavior, the boundaries between appropriate and inappropriate and between acceptable and unacceptable behavior, are therefore different depending on the closeness of the relationship and our own changing perspectives on these matters based on our personal growth.

Unacceptable Behavior and Consequences

As people interact with each other, it is always possible that one or the other will step out of bounds – that is, he violates the unwritten, unspoken and changing rules of the relationship. When that occurs, one of two things will happen.

The first possibility is that a rift will develop and the violation of the boundary lines will be articulated. The person who violated the boundary lines will usually apologize for the misunderstanding or set the record straight as to what actually happened and the motivation for it. In this case, the relationship continues and may actually strengthen as a result of the matter.

A second possibility is that the relationship will be severed. This can be the result if the violation was so serious that no apology or attempt to repair the relationship can be made or if the relationship has suffered from a continued pattern of boundary violations. In short, the person's behavior has become unacceptable.

Based on Trust

As we considered the law and contracts, we noted that these cornerstones of American commerce and economic activity are very formal, documented and specific. By contrast, the standards governing our interpersonal relationships are very poorly defined and tend to vary from one interaction to another. That's because interpersonal relationships are not based on a written code but rather on a nebulous concept called trust.

Trust is the currency of interpersonal relationships. An industrial psychologist who worked with two of the companies one of us has been involved with has an interesting observation about trust. The discussion came up in the context of how management could get the employees to trust them. His observation was this: "You (management) must trust them first."

He went on to explain his view of the dynamics of building trust between two people: I share information with you and, over time, you will come to trust me. In other words, he said, I have to first trust you with information and only then will you begin to trust me. Of course, an underlying assumption is that the information is true; spreading misinformation will have the reverse effect – a lack of trust.

Trust between two people develops as they communicate with each other, interact with each other, and come to rely upon the information they receive from each other.

Trust between an individual and a company works in the same manner. The company must first share information and that information, when tested, must be found to be true.

This is the first rule of ethical business behavior, from the perspective of personal relationships.

We invite you to test this out. Find a company in which the employees don't trust the company or management. Then talk with the people and find out why they don't trust the company. In every case the reason has to do with history: promises that were made, but broken; explanations that were given but turned out to be misleading or incorrect; forecasts about the future that were mistaken. Every item will be a variation on the same theme – information sharing is either non-existent or the information shared was not correct. "They" can't be trusted.

Significance of Personal Relationships in Business

Personal relationships play a very important role in business behavior. They also bring an additional perspective to bear in the evaluation of specific actions as ethical or not.

Almost every activity that a business undertakes involves a personal relationship of some sort. If you are selling the company's products, you are developing personal relationships with your customer's personnel. If you are involved in securing supplies, you probably have some relations with important suppliers. Those involved in hiring personnel have relationships with external recruiters, colleges and universities. In some cases, employees who are producing the product or delivering the service work directly with customer and client personnel. If you are an employee in any capacity, you will have a personal relationship with others in the company.

Additionally, individual employees have personal networks of friends and acquaintances that stretch outside the company's actual sphere of operations. Relationships that are personal networks include people met at trade shows, on the speaking circuit, at conferences and conventions, members of professional organizations, volunteers and board members of charitable organizations, fellow alumni and representatives of colleges and universities.

While these networks are primarily personal in nature, they can convey information about a company and its activities far beyond its immediate customers, suppliers and shareholders. What employees say about the company and their attitude toward their work can speak volumes about what a corporation is really like to others who have no direct involvement with the company.

Finally, inasmuch as a corporation is really an organization of people, every decision having ethical implications is made by one or more individuals, each of whom has her own network of personal relationships within the company, within the company's sphere of operations, within the business or industry community and beyond.

The influence and perspectives of these networks of interpersonal relationships cannot be ignored in the assessment of business behavior. When an employee has a conflict with the company, one he sees as ethical in nature, he may very well take that issue outside the organization for advice, discussion, commiseration and counsel.

When an employee is called upon to do something, he may perceive it as inappropriate, even unethical, separate and apart from any perspective brought to bear by the law, contracts, industry norms and his own professional code of ethics. When that perceived violation of the employee's own boundary lines occurs, the relationship between himself and the organization will become strained and the existence of the perceived violation can become known within and outside of the company.

This presents a challenge for both the employee and the organization. In the employee's view, the organization owes an apology and explanation. In the company's view, the employee's actions may warrant reprimand or dismissal. The trust on which the relationship may be built, however limited, has been broken.

63

Current Ethical Dilemmas Facing Management and Employees

Potential ethical dilemmas are faced every day by employees and others interacting with a business. These conflicts can range from relatively minor to very significant.

Minor violations of trust usually center on a pledge that has been made and then not followed through. A supervisor commits that a person can have a day off, but reneges because a deadline has come up. A person is told that she can have a certain role on a project, but management gives that role to someone else. A group of employees has had a certain set of offices with a nice view for years, and then is asked to move to the basement.

At this level of behavior, company management needs to recognize that a pledge, spoken or unspoken, was made and broken, and then do its best to offer an acceptable alternative. A different day could be taken off, the project role can be modified in a way that challenges the employee, and the department can be given some recognition that offsets the loss of the windows.

Whether or not the company behaved ethically in these situations is a matter of perspective. Few people would say that something truly unethical took place (beyond breaking the implied promise). But morale can be impacted and trust eroded in each case.

More significant conflicts can arise that do indeed pose ethical dilemmas for employees.

- A manager is asked to lay off an employee who is also one of his best friends.
- A favorite co-worker is let go because of a mistake someone else made.
- A supplier is owed money, but the company deliberately delays payment based on tight cash flow. An employee with a longstanding personal relationship with the supplier is told to make up a reason for stalling.
- A sales person commits to a deadline that the product support team knows it cannot make. The support team has had an excellent relationship with the client personnel.

All of these situations can pose problems for employees in dealing with the company because they cross individual boundaries built on personal relationships and trust. In each case the employee is called upon to do something she is unlikely to feel comfortable about.

A company can avoid the first two conflicts by being astute enough to recognize the facts of the situation. In the first case, someone else should be called upon to assist in conveying the layoff news to the manager's friend. In the second case, if the employee comes forward with the facts, the company should take appropriate action, including re-instating the dismissed worker if the person can still work effectively in the organization.

Other situations are more difficult to resolve, particularly if the individuals involved feel uncomfortable in challenging the activity.

In the case of the supplier whose payment is to be delayed, the employee, based on her own upbringing, may feel very uncomfortable about misleading the supplier. At the same time she realizes that if the company's temporary cash flow problems leaked out, other suppliers would tighten credit and demand better terms, thus exacerbating the problem. Also, by giving the supplier a misleading reason for the payment delay, her own future credibility with that organization may suffer.

The product support team has a similar problem. They have had a long relationship with this account and have also developed a relationship of trust. The client personnel have come to know that they can count on this company's product support team. Now the sales person and the company have committed to a deadline that is very unrealistic. The product support people have a dilemma – if they speak up internally, they may suffer political consequences; if they speak up externally they will definitely be in trouble; and if they say nothing the credibility they have worked so hard to establish with the account will be completely at risk.

As can be seen, whenever a company's words or actions fall outside the bounds of truth, complications and dilemmas quickly follow. This is a perspective on ethical behavior that is wrapped up with personal relationships, relationships based on trust, which is based on truth.

Summary

Personal relationships bring a perspective to business activity and actions that is separate and apart from the law, professional codes of ethics and even common business practice. The standards of acceptable and appropriate behavior that people form in their personal relationships are unwritten, vary from relationship to relationship and even change over a person's lifetime. Nonetheless, these standards of behavior, however illusive, are powerful forces that affect not only the company and its employees but extend to others in the community at large and the company's industry and sphere of operations.

How people judge business behavior and determine if it is ethical or not will depend in great part on the relationships they have with the people involved and on how they handle interpersonal relationships themselves. This is particularly true for people who lack knowledge or experience in other backdrops such as the law, professional codes and industry standards.

Corporations and individuals faced with ethical dilemmas should employ the perspective of personal relationships and underlying norms of appropriate behavior in forming judgments about business behavior.

Chapter Eight – The Seventh Layer: Moral and Spiritual Values

Introduction

As noted in the previous chapter, both of the last two views of ethical business behavior – personal relationships and moral and spiritual values - arise from a more individual perspective.

Moral and spiritual values, the focus of this chapter, clearly arise from standards set by more than one person, yet they are also closely associated with individuals. Indeed, spirituality as it is meant here, is highly personal.

Spiritual values often arise from religious instruction, training and upbringing, but in the context of this book we mean the deeply personalized beliefs of the individual, not the collective or authoritarian beliefs of a group. In the context of The Seven Layers of Integrity® model, the collective or authoritarian beliefs of a specific religious group are a part of the layer referred to as the Community Layer, and their relative impact has been described there. Moral and spiritual values more closely resemble what can be called a person's inner conscience or moral compass.

It is the authors' belief that, within the context of the United States *and its business activity*, the moral beliefs of individuals have greater impact on our collective judgment of ethical business behavior than the more formal and often authoritarian perspectives of a religion, denomination or particular church, synagogue or mosque. In judging the ethical conduct of business, our fellow citizens are more likely to respond to the beliefs and opinions of individuals and peers than the beliefs and opinions of the various religions.

What Are Spiritual Values and Moral Values?

Spiritual and moral values arise from a person's most inner belief system. They are focused on the issues of life and death, spiritual existence and one's role in the universe. In particular, they are a system of beliefs about one's role in the world as a human being and what that means regarding our treatment of our self and others.

We are always fascinated at the differences between the spiritual beliefs of individuals and the official promulgations of their own religion or denomination. For example, we know a number of Protestants, Catholics and Jews who believe in re-incarnation – the physical manifestation of one's self in another life as another person. The notion of re-incarnation is not a doctrine of traditional Judaism or Christianity. In fact, the implication that one might get a second, third or any number of additional chances to be good on earth is somewhat contradictory with the single opportunity and subsequent judgment portrayed in both the Old and New Testaments.

Similarly, although there are a great number of Christians who believe that Christianity is the only way to salvation (an official view of Evangelical Christian denominations), there are also large numbers of individual Christians who are much more tolerant and open-minded. They find some value in the other religions and see the good in other human beings.

We, therefore, have come to believe that the spiritual values of most Americans cannot be neatly categorized or described by the official beliefs of their particular proclaimed religion or denomination.

Additionally, increasing numbers of people do not attend or belong to any church, synagogue or mosque, yet have come to believe that there is some form of existence after life. A mutual friend, for example, proclaims herself to be agnostic, yet claims to believe in a hereafter and is open-minded about reincarnation.

An aspect of spiritual and moral values is a focus on how we should treat our self and others. This focus on right and wrong in the real world is sometimes labeled as our moral compass or inner conscience. It is a very personal and inner set of beliefs and core values. The moral compass of an individual has a clear impact on what that person believes to be ethical behavior.

Spiritual and moral values of individuals are often unwritten. Most people do not take time to write down their core beliefs regarding how they should behave and what constitutes right and wrong. A few writers and professional philosophers may do this, but most of us lack the discipline or see the need. Instead, we are content to occasionally articulate or attempt to explain our beliefs, explanations that generally are incomplete and disintegrate under logic. That doesn't make our beliefs any less valid or significant.

However, it does bring us to an interesting point: for many of us, our belief system changes over time. This observation is at odds with common perceptions about Americans held by politicians, the media and business itself. Common belief is that personalities are formed and values solidified at an early age, never to be altered thereafter. "Show me a person's views at age twenty-five and they will be much the same thirty years later." One philosophy goes even further and criticizes those whose values are not constant throughout their lives – in other words, by age twenty-five you should have all the wisdom you'll ever need!

This point of view doesn't pay attention to the facts. Talk with your parents about what they did when they were in their twenties and contrast that with how they behave today. The fact is that people do change over time, even into their later years. They gain experience, they see more of the world, they become more sophisticated, their interests change and the roles they play at home, at work and in the community change as well.

Indeed, those who are most focused on spirituality as an important part of their lives share a common view: spirituality requires continual growth and there is no growth without change. Even those who are not spiritually focused are changing – they just don't fully realize it yet.

Unlike some of the other perspectives on ethical behavior, spiritual values are generally not written, often poorly articulated and constantly changing. This would appear to make them hard to capture as a standard for behavior.

In addition, because these values are very personal and individual, they are not generally enforceable. Unlike the law, contracts, professional codes of ethics and industry standards, moral values lack enforceability in the business world. If an action or activity violates an individual's personal moral values, there is no authority to turn to. Indeed, one of the interesting qualities of moral values is that they are difficult for the individual to impose and enforce upon himself. We are in a constant struggle to be better, a part of the growth process. The values we do articulate are often idealistic and hard to achieve. But that quality makes them so very important.

Moral Values Provide a View of Business Activity

Moral values are important because they represent idealistic views of how we should treat each other. These ideals have the following characteristics:

They take a long-term perspective on life. Spirituality recognizes the possibility that individual lives continue beyond death and that an external force, or Supreme Being, has a long-term involvement with us and with the universe around us. Spiritual people are partly focused on the long-term view.

They hold the lives of individual human beings in the highest of value. Spiritual and moral beliefs focus us on the irreplaceable and precious nature of each human being. Each person is of tremendous value, regardless of his or her apparent outward limitations, be those limitations physical, mental, emotional, psychological, genetic or any other. To paraphrase Jefferson in the Declaration of Independence: All have been endowed by their Creator with certain inalienable rights, among which are life, liberty and the pursuit of happiness.

They acknowledge the innate creativity and potential of people. Most spiritually focused people believe that all of us are in a constant state of growth and that any of us can, with proper opportunity, tap into the creative ideas that come from another source. Indeed, a key part of spiritual growth is the development of our own potential.

They call upon us to set aside ego in the interests of the common good and even the interest of other individuals. Moral and spiritual values call upon us to look outside ourselves and consider the needs of others, individually and collectively. They call upon us to treat our fellow human beings with understanding, forgiveness and love – qualities that reinforce and exceed the notion of respect for others. Fair play falls out of this value, almost as a footnote.

<u>They recognize and value a growth and learning process as an ongoing part of human life.</u> Moral values reinforce the concept of personal growth in all aspects of life. They encourage us to develop all of our potential. They regard growth as a never-ending process; therefore, learning should be continual.

<u>Spiritual and moral values acknowledge the real world as a cherished and important resource that must be nurtured and maintained.</u> There is a sense of obligation and responsibility to future generations that goes beyond development and protection of natural resources to a sense of stewardship.

The above aspects of moral and spiritual values all have implications for any view of ethical business behavior. They set an ultimate standard based on ideals – a standard that no behavior can ever fully measure up to, but that all ethical behavior can reach toward.

In particular, moral and spiritual values reinforce the other perspectives in our model in the following ways:

- The acknowledgement of a Supreme Being or Higher Power focuses us on the moral imperative to obey the law as a minimum standard of behavior.

- The acknowledgement of the value and importance of the needs of others reinforces our recognition of adhering to the contracts and agreements that we have with others, including those that are commitments made personally and without benefit of an executed document.

- The acknowledgement of the need to set ego aside in the interests of others and humanity in general reinforces the professional codes of ethics that call upon professionals to operate above board, open to scrutiny, seeking qualified help when needed, and retaining objectivity and independence.

- The recognition of the importance of continual learning reinforces the professional codes of ethics that call upon us to always apply the best and most current experience to our work.

- The acknowledgement that others share our world and have importance equal to our own reinforces the concept of maintaining standard operating processes within our industry while innovating in creative and constructive ways that increase opportunity for all, instead of stifling competition.

- The acknowledgement of a longer-term view of life reinforces our involvement as active participants in our communities – civic, social and political – with a view to continually improving the human condition. That attempt to improve the human condition drives us to view business activity from an additional perspective in considering whether behavior is ethical or not.

- The acknowledgement of the unique value of each and every human being reinforces the importance of having healthy personal relationships based on mutual trust – relationship values that should be maintained in a business setting.

Moral and spiritual values are the underlying foundation of all the other perspectives in our model. Another way to view this concept is to examine the model and recognize that moral and spiritual values are the foundation and that the other layers are built upon each other until we finally get to the law of the land. The law, in essence, is based upon common notions of how people should treat each other, ideas that are rooted in moral and spiritual beliefs.

Conflicts for Employees

When employees and others are called on to do something that conflicts with their most fundamental moral and spiritual values, conflict will be inevitable. Causing someone to step outside her own inner boundaries of right and wrong will result in at least a feeling of unease and guilt. If the situation is significant or continues for a long time, it is very possible the individual will develop a serious feeling of guilt and anxiety leading to depression or anger.

This inner turmoil will seek resolution. That resolution can consist of any of the following actions: confession, restitution, resignation, mental depression, breakdown, and, in the worst cases, possible suicide attempts.

Confession will involve an admission of perceived guilt, possibly to the injured party but possibly to someone else. The admission may take the details of what happened outside the control of the company involved.

Restitution is an attempt to make good. Acts of restitution could be as simple as an apology or as serious as a discussion with law enforcement about cooperating in an investigation, if the situation involved breaking the law.

Resignation is often an option. An employee may resign in order to take himself out of the situation. This would be a relevant option if the conflict is of an on-going nature or is expected to become one. It would also be appropriate if the employee were being called on to do something illegal.

If the individual keeps the conflict bottled up and becomes obsessive about it, psychological problems could occur including acute depression, anxiety, a mental breakdown or suicide. Executive suicides can occur when the individual feels completely trapped by the situation, is unable to face the personal and family embarrassment associated with his actions, or is faced with testifying against close friends – a sense of betraying others.

Examples of Conflict and Resolution

There are many possibilities for conflict between individuals and a company at a moral level. The obvious ones are situations where the individual has broken a law and faces an enforcement action. However, there are many common situations where employees and others can face a moral dilemma that results from their personal values.

At a previous employer where one of us was in charge of an office of consultants, the company decided to amend the benefits plan to cover domestic partners. A particular consultant found this offensive to his moral values, as it meant recognition of homosexual partners within the benefits program. The employee made the decision to find a new job at an organization that did not have this benefit provision. While we completely disagree with this view of morality and find it totally incompatible with our own sense of moral values, we respect the individual's decision to leave the company.

There are many companies and professions in which the demands on personnel may conflict with moral values with respect to the balance between work and family relationships. These demands include working extraordinary hours on a regular basis and traveling extensively on a regular basis. Many people find this difficult, particularly as they become parents. Single personnel also develop problems with these demands as they find their opportunities for balance limited and begin to see themselves as trapped in a situation in which they will "never meet someone" or "have no life."

Another common conflict is the discovery that the company's culture is not compatible with one's spiritual values. While time and travel also fit this description, so does an excessively dictatorial management style or a style of management that is very intimidating in its handling of people. We personally do not believe that this is an appropriate way to manage people. We also do not see it as a style of management compatible with spiritual values concerning the treatment of others. In a case such as this, the individual's best solution is to find alternative employment at a more compatible organization. Company cultures are usually not changed by a single employee.

Less common situations that pose moral value dilemmas include the perception of fairness in the way in which the company treats its employees, customers, suppliers or the community. For example, if the company's common practice in placing energy trades is to do whatever it takes to gouge the power plants, this may well pose an issue for someone who is asked to participate. Even if the activity is legal, the attitude and outlook toward these captive customers and the knowledge of the impact on the general public could cause someone to perceive this as unethical behavior. In this case, the individual involved may seek to resign.

Summary

Moral and spiritual values are much more difficult to define, enumerate and document than laws, contracts, and professional codes of ethics. An individual's own values may shift over time. Nonetheless, moral and spiritual values play an important role in the determination of ethical behavior.

These values call on us to move to a higher, more ideal level of behavior. Those ideals are impossible for all people to live up to on a consistent basis, but they set a standard that forms the foundation for our overall concepts of right and wrong.

The specific actions and activity of companies and individuals can be examined to determine if they are ethical or not from the perspective of moral values. When an individual comes to believe that his own activity or that of the company is seriously deficient with respect to his personal moral and spiritual values, conflict arises and a resolution of the conflict will be sought.

Conflict resolution in this area can be extreme and will frequently result in an employee resignation after a period of time.

Chapter Nine – Revisiting the Model

Introduction

In Chapter One we introduced The Seven Layers of Integrity® model. The model is intended to provide a number of different perspectives from which business decisions and behavior can be analyzed in an attempt to determine if they are ethical. The subsequent chapters explained these perspectives one by one and provided examples of situations that could present ethical challenges from each layer's perspective.

Each of these perspectives has its validity; each differs from the others; but all are interrelated. In the last chapter we observed that moral and spiritual values are really a foundation for the law and the other layers. This chapter is focused on reviewing the model and demonstrating how it can be used.

Changes in Perspective

You may have noticed that as we crossed The Seven Layers of Integrity® model from Law and Contracts to Spiritual and Moral Values, we changed our perspective in a number of ways.

The Law and Contracts introduced standards of behavior that are well defined and documented. They provide a relatively straightforward way to measure a specific decision, action or activity. The benchmark or standard is clear and our country provides a well-defined system, through attorneys, arbitration panels and the courtroom, to settle the issues. There is an enforcement authority associated with these standards, one that most of us prefer not to cross.

In contrast, we observed that Personal Relationships and Spiritual and Moral Values (1) are not well defined and documented. There is no enforcement system and there is no well-defined arbitration process for disputes in views. Instead, Personal Relationships are built on trust and Spiritual Values are built on beliefs.

Law and Contracts are very specific. They identify specific conditions, stipulate specific actions and take into account specific situations that may occur. By contrast, the standards governing Personal Relationships and Spiritual and Moral Values tend to be more general and fluid, providing broad guidance on how to behave as opposed to specific case-by-case rules.

Obeying the law and honoring written contracts and agreements are the minimum basic requirement of ethical business behavior. Spiritual and moral values comprise an ideal set of behavior, a standard so high that all of us fall short most of the time.

The Validity of Multiple Perspectives

In spite of these apparent contradictions, each of these perspectives has its call on validity. That notion may be objectionable to some readers who believe that there is an ultimate right and wrong and that values should be immutable. But the reality is that our values, individually and as a nation, change over time.

In defense of that statement we suggest readers who have difficulty with the idea of changing values consider the following examples.

At one time, there were a number of states in the United States in which slavery was completely legal and discrimination against an entire race of people was actually defended from the pulpit. Today things are very different. We amended our Constitution as a step to eliminate these wrongs.

At one time, the role of women in the United States was very restricted and those restrictions were strongly defended by the clergy, the press and politicians. Today, women have many more opportunities to participate in society, and the clergy who would like to restrict them to the home are few and far between. The Constitution was amended to provide women with the right to vote.

It is not only a fact of life that our values change; it is often good that they do.

That being said, we should not be timid about accepting the notion that business behavior in particular can be viewed through a number of lenses, each with its own claim on our decisions and judgment and each appropriately vying for its input.

As we move from the minimal requirement to the ideal view of what constitutes ethical behavior, we should always be aware of where we are in the picture, who the lens applies to and how much weight we wish to give to that perspective.

The law is a minimum basic requirement. Ethical behavior in business not only demands that the law be obeyed but also requires that we take steps to know which laws apply to our activities. Formal contracts have the effect of law and should be considered binding. Verbal agreements that both parties understood to be a final deal should be kept in the same fashion.

Professionals who are licensed and certified have an obligation to adhere to their profession's code of ethics. They should take steps to be informed on what those codes are. They should do their best to act in accordance with professional standards at all times. Personnel who are not licensed professionals would do well to become familiar with the concept of professional behavior and strive to follow it.

Companies and their people should always be aware of the standard acceptable practices of their industry. These can be challenged but only in an innovative way, not at the predatory expense of the industry and the nation's commerce.

Civic and political communities have expectations of what constitutes ethical business behavior. When a particular business activity takes the company into the civic and political arena, management should take a good look at their actions through the community's lens. Personal relationships should be valued as well, although there will be times when the legitimate business needs of the company place a lesser weight on these relationships. The personal networks of individuals should be honored and nurtured.

Spiritual and moral values present an ideal that individuals and corporations will be unable to meet at all times. But these values form the basis for much of the general public's sense of right and wrong, even if the public doesn't realize that.

The pyramid found in Diagram 2 presents a different view of The Seven Layers of Integrity® model, a view that recognizes that our ethics structure has spiritual and moral values as the foundation upon which the others rest. In the end, the law is the distilled essence, in writing, of our collective minimum standards based on the other layers and developed through the complex bargaining process called representative democracy.

An Example

The model attempts to present multiple perspectives for examining behavior and passing judgment on whether or not an action is right or wrong, ethical or not.

Consider, for example, an employee of an oil company that has refineries near Houston. The company is considering applying for pollution relief under current state and federal law. The pollution relief is an application for an extension to the deadline by which an older refinery must comply with more recent clean air guidelines. As an employee in the accounting and finance team, he knows that the company has been delaying its upgrade due to a shortage of capital available to make the transition. The current year's earnings could be adversely affected and shareholders could be hurt by a stock pullback. Applying for the extension is not only legal, but the regulations provide for such applications. Moreover, others in the refining industry have likewise been careful about scheduling these outlays and transitioning to the new requirements.

Is the employee doing anything unethical by supporting the application for an extension? The contemplated action by the company will be legal, does not violate any contracts or agreements, and is in line with industry standards of behavior.

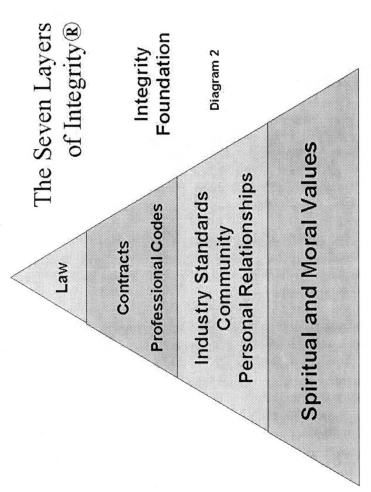

The Seven Layers of Integrity®

Integrity Foundation

Diagram 2

Law

Contracts

Professional Codes

Industry Standards

Community

Personal Relationships

Spiritual and Moral Values

Now let's move to another perspective. The individual is a professional engineer. He knows that the delay in equipment upgrade is a sound financial decision. But as an engineer, he also knows that the expected life of the existing equipment has already been exceeded, maintenance costs (already factored into the economics of the deal) are increasing and so is the risk that a significant problem will develop, one that could release tons of toxic chemicals into the atmosphere.

Is the employee being unethical by supporting the application for extension? What does the professional code of ethics for engineers have to say?

Now consider another factor. The employee lives within a ten-mile radius of the facility. He is part of the local community that would be impacted by an accident, and is already affected by continuing the current (legal) level of emissions. So without an accident, his family and neighbors are continuing to breathe air that could be somewhat cleaner if the upgrade were made now instead of later. How does he view the company's ethical behavior now?

And finally, let's consider that the engineer is the father of a newborn child. He and his wife are very concerned about the long-term health impact on their infant of continuing to live this close to the facility. Is his support of the extension ethical?

We use this example to illustrate how our thinking can indeed change as we move through these different layers or perspectives. In a way, it is similar to visiting the optometrist and looking through the device that helps identify the exact prescription for your new lenses. The first view (obey the law) is reasonable enough, but not sharp and clear. If you had to, you could survive with this prescription, but it would be uncomfortable. Successive changes improve the clarity of what you see, until the final prescription (spirituality) makes everything crystal clear.

Herein lies the transition from merely obeying the law to doing what is best for our planet and the people on it.

Footnotes

(1) The reader may argue that organized religion provides a well-defined and documented set of standards for moral and spiritual values. However, within the context of this model we have positioned organized religions as a part of the Community layer and have reserved Spiritual and Moral Values as a layer that is oriented to core spiritual beliefs.

Chapter Ten – Current Litigation Issues

Introduction

Now that we have explored The Seven Layers of Integrity® in the context of business ethics, we will examine recent business activity, using the model to identify potential ethical problems. With the law as our common starting position, our baseline of measurement of ethical business behavior, we will first explore some of the common litigation issues for business in today's environment. The following chapters will consider ethical issues and corporate cultures, specific ethical considerations in the age of electronic communication and surveillance, and conclude by examining the role of individual responsibility within the context of an organization.

Common Areas of Litigation

Discrimination and Sexual Harassment

While not making the news as much as it once did, racial and gender discrimination in business is still an issue, and an important legal and ethical matter.

Discrimination is clearly against the law. There are federal and state laws that apply to discrimination and sexual harassment in the workplace. Companies and individuals can be and have been sued for this behavior.

Discrimination in any form is also unethical. Discrimination essentially robs the individual of his or her opportunity to contribute. It says that what you are capable of doing today and what you can learn to do tomorrow are diminished by the color of your skin, your gender, your religion, or your personal attractiveness. This discrimination is at odds with any enlightened view of life. It is fundamentally at odds with the underlying premise of American democracy: "All men are created equal." And "men," if Jefferson were alive today, would likely have been written as "people."

Equality of all people is the basis for everything else we hold dear as a country. It is intricately tied to our beliefs in freedom of speech, freedom of religion, personal liberties, and the right to start a business and to own property. In the end, these rights to prosper and progress enhance our economic and social progress as a nation. Such rights are a source of innovation and creativity vital to maintaining prosperity.

At the same time, we live in a nation where not everyone has come up to speed on these important truths. We also grow up culturally indoctrinated to categorize people based on outward characteristics, limiting our perception of their capabilities before they even start.

Racial discrimination still exists in our country, although it is often subtle and more likely to be regarded as wrong when exposed. Racial discrimination in the workplace is no longer officially accepted, although there have still been some relatively recent and significant charges against major corporations, government agencies and retail establishments.

Sexual discrimination in the workplace and sexual harassment are still all too common. Women have difficulty getting into some industries and even when they have jobs they are often excluded from male oriented camaraderie that builds vital future personal relationships and networks. The glass ceiling is still very much in existence, although a few more women have become CEOs of large companies (Hewlett-Packard, Lucent and E-bay). Sexual discrimination can still be embedded in the culture of an organization, even those organizations that portray themselves as more enlightened, such as some of our universities.

Every organization has an obligation to protect workers from discrimination and harassment. Formal corporate policies should be documented and effectively communicated to all employees. Supervisors and managers should be on the alert to discover discriminatory acts and respond to suspected violations quickly and fairly. Training, particularly training concerning harassment, should be provided to all employees.

From a perspective of professional ethics and conduct, no excuse exists for discrimination and harassment. Professional personnel should conduct themselves in an appropriate manner.

From a perspective of spiritual and moral values, these actions are clearly unethical.

Financial Disclosure and Fraud

The most obvious current ethical problem for corporate America is proper financial disclosure and financial fraud. Consider that problem as we examine it using each of The Seven Layers of Integrity®.

In financial fraud cases, the general public does not always know when the law has been actually broken; the accounting rules and SEC regulations are complex and technical. It is clear however, that the ethical perspective of the investing public, one of the Community groups we discussed, has been very different from the perspectives of the investment industry and accounting professionals. Let's examine the perspectives of each of the Seven Layers, beginning with the Law.

As noted, the relevant law is complex and not well known. Since people need to understand legal requirements in order to obey them, opportunities exist for individuals to be unaware of the implications of their actions. Nonetheless, senior executives have the responsibility to know the regulations; therefore, when these executives violate the law, their ethics and integrity are rightfully called into question.

From the perspective of the second layer, Contracts and Agreements, companies have no formal agreements with shareholders and the investing public, aside from the company's articles of incorporation and by-laws. However, in recent cases, some understandings were violated, particularly the public's understanding that companies would represent their financial results fairly and accurately and that independent auditors would test that accuracy and representation, and report appropriately to the public. In that regard, the public trust, that unwritten agreement between shareholders and management, has definitely been violated.

As we move to the perspective of professional codes of ethics, the violation of standards for ethical behavior become clear. The codes of the accounting profession, as promulgated by the profession through the State Boards of

Public Accountancy, were clearly violated by corporate CFOs (most CFOs are CPAs) in a number of instances.

More troubling is the behavior of the external audit firms. Had they known all the facts, an auditing firm should not have given HealthSouth, Worldcom or Adelphia clean bills of health. The unethical behavior on the part of the audited companies would have been clearly seen. But in a number of cases it appears that the audit firms, knowing a part of the story, failed to assert their professional obligations and instead may have worked to bend the rules in order to give their clients a stamp of approval.

Considering the fourth layer, Industry Standards, the standards themselves seem to have taken a step downward with respect to this issue. It appears that inaccurate financial disclosure, misleading financial analysis and hyping stocks that were not worth the suggested value were all commonplace occurrences in the investment banking community. Moreover, it would appear that within certain industries, such as energy trading, the reporting of misleading numbers was common practice.

Whenever industry standards lead to violations of the law, the standards themselves were unethical. But for people insulated in these industries, surrounded every day by these on-going practices, not questioning the ethics of their practices became the norm.

Within the Community layer, the investing public, once knowledgeable of the facts, began to clearly see the ethical problems in companies' and industries' behaviors. As a result, the investment banking industry lost the public's trust. Financial advisors lost the public's confidence. And as the financial statements of the largest corporations became questionable, with restatements of balance sheets in the news, the accounting profession lost its reputation for integrity.

The spiritual and moral principles of honesty and stewardship were clearly violated.

Gaming the System

"Gaming the system" is a phrase that describes a business activity in which companies take advantage of flawed processes or complex systems to exploit their less knowledgeable customers.

Gaming the system has become prevalent in two industries, to the detriment of the general public and the nation's economy.

The financial investment industry developed an approach to the estimation and reporting of quarterly earnings. The way the game worked was basically as follows. A publicly held company would report its quarterly earnings and then also give forward looking projections on its business conditions for the next quarter, current fiscal year and next fiscal year. The financial analysts would then estimate the earnings for the next quarter. The financial analysts' estimates were published and tracked on numerous publicly available stock tracking Internet sites. Investors would then expect that the company's next quarter results would fall within a particular range. The company realizes that lesser results (and sometimes even results within the bottom end of the range) would potentially be disappointing and drive down the stock price. The company, therefore, worked to massage its numbers so that reported earnings for that range fell into the top half of the financial analysts' projections, or better still beat those projections by a penny or two. Everyone was happy. The financial analysts looked smart because their projections were on target. The company was happy because a bad quarter did not occur. Investors were happy because the company's growth rate appeared to be steady or improving. This was the game.

The game broke down as the economy slowed and went into a recession. Numbers could not be made. Some companies reported lesser earnings and their stock prices were slammed. Other companies began (or continued!) to stray outside the bounds of accounting principles so their numbers could be made. Eventually they all paid the piper. As real numbers surfaced, many companies went back several *years* to restate their prior results. Now we are in a period where no one trusts anyone's numbers.

Another industry that appears to have gamed the system was energy trading.

During the height of the California energy crisis, when California faced rolling blackouts and Pacific Gas and Electric (PG&E) was rapidly running out of cash to buy power, several energy trading companies are now alleged to have gamed the system. Recognizing that PG&E would have to buy additional power on the spot market, and that spot market prices were based on total demand, company energy traders filled the system with fictitious trades, selling power back and forth to each other to drive the price up.

It is not clear if the energy traders broke any existing laws (although conspiracy conceptually could be one). It is clear that they took advantage of the California predicament. Did they behave ethically?

Let's assume no laws were broken. The contracts they had with PG&E may have been followed (that too will be up to the courts to decide). Indeed, the energy trading industry seemed to accept this behavior. That leads us to professional codes of ethics and community standards as our measurement perspectives. Energy traders do not seem to have a professional code of ethics. The codes of ethics of most professions address pricing in some form; some address price fixing and competitive bidding. It is fair to say that in the eyes of most professions this kind of activity, working the system to drive the price up by creating demand when there was none, would be unethical.

Certainly as we move to community standards we begin to find a clear view of the activity that went on. We believe that as the facts come out in further investigations, it will be clear that gaming the system to artificially drive up spot prices was unethical business behavior and will result in regulation to punish that type of activity.

Environmental Litigation

Protecting the environment is a cause that draws passionate supporters from many walks of life all across the country. It is an issue that the social community in our Community Layer focuses on.

Corporations face other issues. They need to be profitable, competitive, efficient and growing. When the environment becomes a part of their sphere of operations, conflict frequently occurs.

We can see the different perspectives on this as we move from one layer to another. A company may be adhering to current environmental law, but still be seen as a polluter in the eyes of the local community. Most companies cannot make a case that they are focused on being true stewards of the earth – the idealistic spiritual view of ethical behavior.

Our view of a company's actions is also often tainted by how it conducts itself when under fire. If the passionate environmentalists think the company is not being responsive, then they and many others may conclude that ethical behavior is lacking, even though the organization is obeying the law and making some effort to improve its operations.

The best way to approach this challenge is to be open and above board with the facts. Explain the rationale for current approaches and the timetables for any planned improvements. Increased credibility rarely occurs when information is withheld.

Use of Insider Information in Stock Trades

The use of insider information to make money on the stock market is another current issue. The law in this regard is clear – insider information is clearly defined and the law clearly states that it is a punishable offense, with potentially significant penalties.

When insiders within a publicly traded company are allocated stock options or the right to otherwise acquire company shares, they are apprised of the conditions surrounding the purchase and sale of company stock. The company is required to report all stock transactions of its insiders.

The company does not have control, however, over non-employees who become aware of inside information and seek to profit by it.

Insider information is essentially knowledge of some financial transaction or other news that would affect the stock price of a company but is not publicly disclosed. For example, the news that a poorly performing plant will be closed or a subsidiary sold could impact a company's stock in a positive direction. During the period of time that this news is unavailable to the general public, an employee with the company or its legal or financial advisors may illegally make use of that knowledge to attempt to trade at a profit. Other kinds of news could cause the stock to drop.

In several recent cases, individuals allegedly may have been privy to insider information from people or clients with whom they did business. By disposing of shares ahead of bad news, a financial loss was averted when this news became public and other investors began selling. By acquiring shares ahead of positive announcements, financial gains were achieved.

The use of insider information, as defined in the Securities and Exchange laws of the United States, is illegal and therefore clearly unethical. We could do a better job of educating the average investor about these laws and the definition of inside information. Someone could think that everyone else knew the information he or she was given, even though that was not the case. The deliberate use of insider information by a person who knows the information falls into that category is clearly unethical.

This behavior violates the professional code of ethics for anyone who in the accounting profession or legal profession. It violates community political standards in that it strikes at the heart of the notion of a level playing field in the equity markets. It violates professional standards because it is illegal.

Summary

The most common areas of litigation with respect to business ethics today have common threads and they are found in the corporate culture. Corporate culture contributes to an atmosphere of discrimination and harassment. A culture that overly focuses on revenue and stock price growth causes employees to reach to greater extremes, actions that may overstep the law, in order to produce the desired results. A casual attitude toward securities laws as they affect individual investment decisions results in overstepping the bounds in making one or more key decisions.

In many of these cases, the evolving culture of the organization or industry is partly to blame for the ultimate acceptance of illegal activity. We need to be much more focused on building cultures that have zero tolerance for violation of the law and a greater emphasis on good corporate and individual citizenship.

Corporate culture and business politics is our next topic.

Chapter Eleven – Corporate Culture and Business Ethics

Introduction

Those who have had careers in the broader business world, whether in a large corporation or a small non-profit organization, know that the most common tests of our own ethical values in business are found in playing the politics that is associated with being part of an organization.

While business politics may be something we would like to leave behind, politics is simply a natural part of human relationships. Were there no hierarchical structures and no bosses, politics would still develop. Leaders would emerge and vie for influence. Cooperation would evolve into "you do this for me now and I will do something for you later" – the basic nature of politics. Business politics are inevitable.

Business politics do not play out in a vacuum, nor do they reach the same results in one company versus another. Like a fish in the aquarium, politics lives within a culture – the company's culture.

Business Politics and Business Decisions

We all know that politics can influence business decisions. Indeed, the process of reaching business decisions always has political considerations from start to finish. While CEOs would like to think that they can order and employees will obey, the truth is that employees obey with varying degrees of enthusiasm and cooperation depending on whether or not they are in agreement with the company's direction.

Often the influence of politics and culture can cause a company to do something that is less than efficient or effective. Sometimes the influence of politics and culture can cause a company to do something that is less than ethical.

Corporate politics can be nefarious in the way individuals may be influenced to do things that are less than ethical. Should we really follow through on that promise we made at the last steering committee meeting or should we let it die a quiet death now that we know a certain VP is against it? Should we share that confidential piece of information regarding Sally's last performance appraisal? Should we call that bothersome account and try to make its relationship with us so unpleasant that the account will walk away from us? In truth, few of us make a conscious decision to do something unethical – we simply get there by many minute steps, crossing the boundary by just a hair.

How Culture Influences Politics

The culture of a business organization sets the tone for its politics. In organizations that value open communication and feedback, a relationship of trust and an outlook of bringing problems to attention so they can be resolved tends to prevail. In that kind of environment, politics tends to take a back seat to doing the best thing based on the known facts.

On the other hand, a culture that involves constant pressure to perform, a disregard for past achievements and a strictly bottom line focus, can lead to an atmosphere in which everyone is trying to make his numbers at all costs. In that culture, politics will play a heavy role in everything that goes on.

In a culture where there is complete disregard for workers versus management, a "them versus us" mentality can quickly arise. That type of environment can lead to a complete lack of open and honest communication and even an outright attempt by employees to sabotage management's efforts.

A culture that involves rewarding *rainmakers* (personnel functioning principally in a revenue generating mode who bring in large revenue dollars) above all others will often lead to an organization where revenue numbers are hyped or inflated; contract terms are less than profitable in order to secure the sale; and unethical practices begin to arise. Typical unethical practices associated with such cultures involve the types and magnitude of favors granted to large customers, the timing of accounting for revenue on the books, and the policies and decisions made with respect to customers and sales personnel.

In short, what the company rewards and values is often what they get. Reward intimidation and everyone will be an intimidator of someone else. Reward revenue and everyone will try to get revenue at all costs. Reward cost cutting and you often end up with an organization filled with less expensive employees who are usually less skilled. Foster a win-lose mentality and you can get an organization whose customers and suppliers are its enemies.

Culture and Politics Impact Ethical Behavior

What you reward or value is what you usually get. Similarly, what management focuses on is what people pay attention to.

When decisions are made, does anyone ask, "Is this ethical?" In most companies, this question has been rarely asked.

Culture and politics can produce a combination that can be aggressively hostile to ethical behavior or subtly in conflict with ethical behavior. Two examples that illustrate these ideas are Enron and Arthur Andersen.

As Enron adopted elements of the McKinsey culture (such as the forced ranking of employees against each other, or "rank and yank"), management also appears to have become very aggressive in dealing with employees and outsiders who challenged them. The Enron culture placed a very heavy emphasis on loyalty, rewarded rainmakers with large bonuses and stock options, and put down those who did not "get" the game plan and the corporate strategy. In so doing, a behavior pattern commenced in which questionable acts of top executives and managers went largely unchallenged. The few, such as Sherron Watkins, who did challenge accounting and other practices, were sometimes aggressively dealt with by being cut out of the information loop, receiving hits on their performance reviews from people they had not directly worked for and having their careers flatten out. The organization's culture caused them to be marginalized.

In the case of Arthur Andersen & Co., the accounting firm that audited Enron, the shift in focus from valuing objectivity, integrity and professional reputation to generating revenue, created a subtler, but highly effective, challenge. The one partner who challenged the accounting treatment Enron wanted to use for off-balance sheet partnerships became a problem for Enron. When Enron executives requested his removal from their account, Andersen decided to go along with the request. The ethical conflicts involved were overshadowed by the desire to generate revenue. Enron was one of the firm's most lucrative U.S. clients. The organization was able to rationalize why its client's accounting treatment for the off-balance partnerships was acceptable and honored the request to remove the person who was challenging the appropriateness of that accounting.

Business culture is indeed a powerful force with far reaching impact. That impact has the potential for being manifested in unethical behavior. Here are some additional examples to illustrate that concept.

Management Decisions: Nuclear Power Plant

The impact of business culture and politics on ethical management decisions is found in the story of the Davis-Besse nuclear reactor near Toledo, Ohio (as reported in *The New York Times* (1)).

In 1988, a report prepared by a former Nuclear Regulatory Commission inspector concluded that conflicts between management and the workers had reached a point where management was not in touch with the plant's condition. According to the report, management apparently "disdained" its employees and discounted their concerns about the facility's safety.

The report stated that "Many craft personnel hold strong negative perceptions of engineering and management personnel" and that "the labor forces feel that management exhibits a general lack of concern or respect for their abilities, efforts or problems."

The report identified issues in the relationship between management and employees that led to reluctance on the part of operations and maintenance personnel to bring problems to management's attention. Management was allegedly "unwilling" to consider those problems.

According to *The New York Times'* story, top executives at the time ordered the report's author to change his report. "They just didn't want to hear it," he was quoted as saying in an interview.

Coincidentally with the lack of open communication with maintenance and operations personnel, a serious corrosion problem went undiscovered until February of 2002, at which point there was the very real possibility of a rupture in the reactor vessel, a potentially dangerous situation.

In this example, the one specific decision that was unethical, asking the investigator to change his report, was the culmination of other, more tolerable decisions. The corrosion in the reactor vessel may very well have **not** been present at the time of the investigation. But the day-to-day decisions by management in their handling of communication with employees and the messages they must have given in considering employee concerns worked over a period of time to build an internal cultural barrier to frank communication. Those messages, like the dripping Boron that ate away the steel, steadily eroded management's access to the facts necessary to uphold its responsibilities to the company and to the public. In the end, this lack of professional ethical behavior in dealing with employees affected plant safety far more significantly than the request to change the investigator's report.

Management Decisions: The Challenger Disaster

Many of us still remember where we were and what we were doing when we heard the news that America's Space Shuttle Challenger had exploded during its launch. As weeks and months went by, an extensive investigation uncovered the root cause: a problem with the seals between the massive parts of the exterior fuel tanks. When exposed to a cold enough temperature, these seals became brittle, cracked and resulted in the explosion.

As with many disasters that take place involving a piece of equipment that was used successfully multiple times before, the potential risk of catastrophe had been previously identified and was known to engineering personnel. A warning about the overnight temperatures at the launch site had actually been given by one engineer and was forwarded upward through the decision making structure.

Unlike the culture associated with the Davis-Besse nuclear reactor, the NASA culture was much more open, communicative and tuned in to safety issues. Nevertheless, the decision making process failed due to a cultural shift that occurred over several years.

At its inception, NASA was a relatively small organization with a 'gung-ho' positive attitude. It had a mission – to put a man on the moon and bring him safely back to earth within only ten years from starting. The highly talented and dedicated team assembled for this task worked with a definitive sense of purpose. The stakes were high: America's prestige was on the line, and so was a perceived risk to our national defense if the Soviet Union achieved technological superiority in the space race.

But after the lunar missions were completed and the Soviets gave up trying to get to the moon, NASA lost its sense of definitive purpose. A well-tuned and very close group of people became a large bureaucracy with many contractors vying for business and a very detailed procurement and management process. Levels of management and a complex organization structure slowed down key decisions.

The decision regarding the O-Rings needed to be made quickly. It was a risk that had to be weighed against other pressing concerns, including an ambitious series of on-going shuttle launches, the agency's overall issues with Congress and many other factors. Somewhere along the trail, the concern about the O-Rings diminished in importance and dropped from the list of issues considered in the final launch decision made that morning.

There was probably no one point along the way, no one person that consciously decided to go with the launch in the full knowledge of the potential for disaster. But collectively, as an organization, that decision was in fact made.

It would be unfair to characterize this decision as unethical because it did not violate the standards of any of the seven perspectives we have looked at. The engineer who was aware of the problem reported it. Had he not, we could say that he violated his professional code. No one blocked the reporting of his concern. Had someone done so, we could say that he behaved unethically. What happened was truly a tragic mistake.

Yet the lesson of Challenger is just as real in understanding the way in which other organizations can sometimes make a clearly unethical decision. Step by step, from one level to another, from one part of the organization to another, through conflicting political and business priorities, the ethical significance of the contemplated action is lost, in much the same way as the safety risk of the O-Rings was lost at NASA.

Years later, in 2003, a second shuttle was tragically lost. As the investigative reports were reaching their initial conclusions, one of those conclusions was that the safety mechanisms created following the Challenger disaster were starved of funding during the intervening years. (2) Once again, culture and politics enabled a series of incremental decisions to be made that overlooked a significant safety concern.

Footnotes

(1) " '88 Warning Was Rejected at Damaged Nuclear Plant," *The New York Times*, September 30, 2002, page A14.
(2) "When Astronauts Were in Peril," *The New York Times* (Editorial), May 16, 2003, page A26.

Chapter Twelve – Electronic Issues

Background and Current Status

Electronic communication, particularly the use of e-mail and the Internet, has become widespread during the past decade. Many companies have encountered significant issues in dealing with e-mail and other forms of communication and a number of these issues have ethical implications.

Prior to electronic communication, only written documents and verbal discussions were media for communicating in the business world. While the advent of the telegraph in the last century began an electronic based communication method, the telegraph left no footprints, save the written documents at each end. The electrons traveled down the highway and disappeared.

Tape recording became a business tool in the post World War II era, and tape recording was the first step into some of our current issues. As President Nixon discovered, tape recording of conversations means that verbal discussions have an existence and life of their own, one that is not always controllable. While the infamous eighteen minute gap in one of the Watergate related tapes was not recoverable, its existence was all too visible. Moreover, the tape itself was a physical item that could be discovered by court order and listened to by unintended parties – people who had not been privy to the original verbal discussion.

In many ways, subsequent electronic media have posed similar problems. In addition, modern technology makes it possible to recover items that were erased, enables the automatic archiving of copies of erased material, leaves an incredible log or audit trail of the modifications that may have been made, including deletion, and points to a computer and/or user identification of the source of each document's creation, modification and attempted destruction. All of these copies and logs are subject to subpoena and computer experts can review and analyze all of the trails that were left behind.

Document recovery through the use of archives, or off-site backups, figured prominently in another political scandal – the Iran Contra affair. A White House operative deleted his copies of some documents, but failed to realize that in the intervening months between their origin and destruction, routine backups to off-site locations had created recoverable copies.

In addition, our current Internet environment with fire walls protecting us from external viruses and hackers and additional internal servers storing and routing traffic means that the location of copies of any e-mail and attached documents are numerous. Since each copy is a magnetically encoded set of data, mere deletion of the item is not sufficient. Each and every electronic duplicate must be tracked down and the physical location of its magnetic bits must be overwritten. Although software products exist that can perform these overwrites, the prospect of completely covering one's trail is virtually impossible.

E-mail that is sent outside the company can also be routed via the Internet to an essentially random and unknown set of intermediary locations. The very concept of the original Internet was to have multiple paths for these communications, paths that could be configured and changed by the network itself, so that a nuclear attack on the U.S. could not destroy the entire electronic infrastructure. Today, with traffic high and an ever increasing number of users, sophisticated routing equipment located literally all over the globe switches messages and even parts of messages from one location to another to achieve the fastest possible transmission. A trail of that message is left on every server along the way.

In an interesting sort of way, our own technology has become similar to earlier versions of God – an entity that hears our every electronic communication and records it somewhere just in case we try to fib.

Most people who use e-mail and process electronic documents do not realize how extensive this network is and how impossible it would be to erase their electronic and magnetic fingerprints.

Common Pitfalls of Electronic Communication

E-mail and other forms of electronic communication are virtually impossible to erase or conceal. In addition, they are virtually impossible to control.

As we all have experienced, an e-mail sent to only one person can end up in almost anyone's possession. For one thing, it is so incredibly easy to forward an e-mail to others. And the entire text is automatically sent – you don't even have to walk down the hall to the copy machine. E-mail can be forwarded when you reply to someone. And when you reply, you can add others to the recipient list. That means that the original communiqué goes with your reply to the new people on the list. That is not always a good thing.

In fact, e-mails often contain an entire volley of back and forth discussion from other people. If you had the time or inclination, you could go down to the end and work your way forward. In this fashion, a person who was not privy to the original electronic discussion can read it all if the original parties involved are careless enough. That is not always a good thing either.

E-mails received by other people can also be posted in various places. Recipients can copy all or portions of the original. Those copies can land on electronic bulletin boards, show up in databases, and find their way into memos and company discussion groups. Consider the following incident that occurred a few years ago. A small publicly held company with regional offices had one of its executives show up at the Midwest location. The exec observed that the parking lot was devoid of cars prior to eight am and after five-thirty pm. He then sent out an e-mail to his direct reports at that location, noting this matter and strongly implying that the office was not serious enough about getting its work done. Somewhere along the way, the e-mail slipped into the hands of the employees who promptly and irately sent it to each other. One employee sent the e-mail or a copy of it into an external bulletin board used by stock investors. Within twenty-four hours, the company's stock took a ten percent dive. Investors did not like the tone of the e-mail and the perceived impact on employee morale.

The privacy of e-mails for some reason is far less regarded than that of a letter. Consider, for example, that you receive a hand written letter from a personal friend. Would you think about copying that letter and sending it to other friends? Would you consider sending it to people who weren't in a common circle of friends? Most of us would not do such a thing with a letter we receive in the regular mail. But we will readily, almost unthinkingly, do those things with an e-mail, even one that contains sensitive material.

An additional problem with e-mail in particular is that the tone of the communication is often not what you really intended. We have all seen cases where an e-mail we sent raised the hackles of its recipient unexpectedly. Partly this is because e-mails are so easy to send. Partly it is a reflection of our own torrid pace – we lack the time to plan what we say and instead just dash off our reaction or advice or commentary.

But there is one other, and significant reason for problems with our tone. E-mail is a one-way dialogue. Unlike normal human conversation, face-to-face or even over the telephone, e-mail does not give you a chance to observe the reaction of your listener while you are still in mid-sentence. It doesn't give you a chance to catch the mood of the person before you begin. And with many people checking their e-mails on a continual basis (an inefficient habit) your recipient may also have been caught in the middle of an important crisis that colors his perception of what you are trying to say.

In summary, the common pitfalls of e-mail communication are:

1. The e-mail can be readily created and sent
2. It can be easily copied
3. You cannot control where it goes or who sees it
4. It cannot be completely deleted from our electronic networks
5. It is a discoverable document in any legal inquiry
6. The communication tone, real or perceived, can easily be out of synch with your intentions

Legal Implications for Electronic Communication

As noted, electronic communication is a discoverable document. This fact is worthy of some further discussion, as it poses ethical challenges with respect to the appropriate handling of e-mail.

During the discovery period that preceded the trial involving Microsoft and the Attorneys General of many states, e-mails came out that had been written by Mr. Gates and Mr. Ballmer. These e-mails were potentially damaging to Microsoft and a number of them were published in the press. What may have seemed as relatively innocent, but earnest, exhortations to be competitive in the market place had the potential to be viewed as directives to eliminate the competition in an allegedly illegal manner.

One of the authors of this book was employed by a company that became involved in legal action with a client and as a result had an opportunity to see first hand how some of the e-mails personnel had written could be misconstrued in a trial. Along the way, the project team had difficulties with a particular software component. Frustration ensued and a couple of heated e-mails were exchanged back and forth among team members. It was never expected that these e-mails might become involved in a lawsuit at the time they were written. But the opposing legal team, upon discovery of these e-mails, attempted to use them to build its case against the company.

In particular, a number of the above pitfalls exacerbated the situation:

- The e-mails were written in haste from one team member to another;
- The e-mails contained a tone that was probably intended as sarcastic but, in black and white, appeared to be factually critical;
- The e-mails became discoverable; and
- The copies of the discovered e-mails were, in a few cases, not actually in the hands of those who had the electronic conversation, indicating the e-mails had moved outside of the control of the project team.

Every company has an ethically legitimate need to educate its employees in the proper use of e-mail communication. In the above situation it would have been far more appropriate for the team to not pass sarcastic mail back and forth. The legitimate issues with the software could have been discussed in a conference room and documentation (meeting agenda and minutes) could have indicated simply the facts of the matter, optional courses of action and actual resolution. Following this particular legal problem, our internal counsel did in fact have a training session with the managers in the company.

Given the litigious modern business environment, any e-mail you create should be considered as an item that could appear tomorrow in *The New York Times*. These communications, similar to written memoranda, should be carefully written, clearly thought through, and regarded as company property. Employees should be carefully educated about corporate e-mail and documentation policies and in particular should understand that corporate e-mail is company property, confidential in nature and not to be published externally without appropriate authorization. Discipline is often swift in these cases, but having to discipline at all means you have already been embarrassed or worse.

A further legal issue for electronic communication is the privacy and confidentiality of the content. While this is an issue for print documents as well, electronic forms of information have created additional risks for maintaining privacy and confidentiality.

A recent example of a potential legal issue with respect to privacy was the situation in which the personnel in the admissions office of a major university used applicant social security numbers to access the database of the admissions office of a competing university. The purpose was allegedly to ascertain if the competing university was going to issue an acceptance to the candidate.

Both parties in this situation had legal as well as ethical exposure. The intruding university's admissions application most likely indicated the purposes for which the applicant's social security number would be used. Prying into the competitor's database was probably not one of those proposed uses.

At the same time, the competing university may have some exposure in terms of how relatively easy it was for its applicant database to be hacked into. Maintaining the confidentiality and protecting the privacy of the students' information was potentially compromised on both sides of the situation.

Companies have a legal obligation to safeguard information, particularly the private and confidential data of individuals. Recent regulations in this regard are undoubtedly just the beginning. An excellent example of what lies ahead can be found in new federal regulations for the healthcare industry concerning the protection of individual medical records. Called the Healthcare Information Protection and Portability Act, or HIPPA, these rules call for a very comprehensive safeguard of certain patient electronic data, including audit trails of who accessed it, who maintained it, who backed it up, where it went and who accessed the computer rooms where the database servers are physically located.

Ethical Issues for Electronic Data and Communication

Having outlined the basic pitfalls and legal issues surrounding electronic communication and documentation, we now focus on some of the specific ethical issues that can arise with electronic communication.

Document Discovery

It should go without saying that once an investigation is in process, document shredding and the deletion of electronic files are totally unethical. They are most likely illegal, depending on the actual actions taken and their timing. A central part of the government's action against Arthur Andersen & Co. was centered on Andersen's document shredding, which included electronic copies. Document destruction was also a key issue in the government's prosecution of former Silicon Valley investment banker Joe Quattrone.

In addition to its likely illegality, document destruction cannot really be successful. We outlined earlier in this chapter the myriad ways in which the electronic copies can proliferate themselves and still be found. These attempts will never be successful in today's technology environment, as Andersen quickly discovered.

Therefore, you should regard any electronic item as fully discoverable in the case of legal action against your company or yourself.

We believe it is totally ethical to educate people concerning the law, the issues regarding document discovery and the types of ways that seemingly innocent material can be inadvertently harmful. It is totally ethical to have written company policies concerning the appropriate and inappropriate content that should be conveyed in electronic format. It is totally ethical to tell employees that any e-mail communication from them should be clearly written, factually accurate and professional in style and tone. It is ethical to tell employees that verbal communication is still allowed in the electronic age.

Privacy Protection

Due care should always be taken with respect to the private information of individuals. Examples of this kind of information include employee performance evaluations and compensation, client confidential information, customer financial data, credit card information, credit history data, medical history data, and any form of personal identification (such as social security number and driver's license).

Information systems constructed to process and maintain this type of data must be appropriately secure and safeguarded. They should be designed to prevent intrusion from either external or internal sources.

Employees should be trained in privacy issues and company policies should be clear about the appropriate and inappropriate handling of private information. In some cases, discipline should include immediate dismissal.

Electronic Snooping

While situations such as the university admissions hacking incident described above are rarely in the news, there is every reason to suspect that this kind of snooping occurs more often. Attempting to electronically acquire competitor and customer confidential data by using the Internet to hack into confidential databases and computer servers is clearly unprofessional and unethical.

Using legitimate information is fine. Legitimate information is information your competitor publishes on its public web site, publishes in various print media, or doesn't consider confidential. Information about your competitor that appears in any public media, such as the newspaper, popular magazines and cable networks is legitimate. Information gleaned from a third party that is a research firm is legitimate.

The basic question should be this – was the data acquired or accessed from public sources and third parties who make it available to others in a public way? Was it obtained through your own internal research using legitimate sources? If it was not obtained via legitimate channels, then there is an ethics question for the company to resolve.

Copyright Violations

It used to be hard to steal someone's music, business process, or written work. The electronic age has made that all too easy. People are able to download, copy, distribute and replicate music, photos, text, charts, logos, and anything else they can find over the Internet without regard to copyright restrictions.

The music industry in particular has been very concerned about this capability. Regardless of your opinions of the industry, its treatment of artists and its pricing structure, copyright protected material is essentially the private property of a company and/or individual(s). If you wouldn't steal their car, you shouldn't steal their music, even if you can.

The same is equally true for the copyright protected material of writers, publishers, graphic artists, photographers and other owners of copyright and/or trademark protected intellectual property.

Using copyright protected material without permission and/or acknowledgement is unethical behavior.

Personal Use of Corporate Resources

Office workers often forget that a desktop computer and its software and Internet access capability belong to the company they work for. Most companies now have a written policy with respect to the use of the desktop and Internet for personal matters. You should get a copy of that policy and read it. Then follow it.

If the policy does not address time spent at the office surfing the Net, it should. Recent studies have shown that Internet surfing is one of corporate America's biggest time wasters. Time is money and you are being paid to do something else.

The use of company resources, including yourself, for personal matters or a personal business is neither professional nor ethical.

Electronic Crime

A whole new area for law enforcement is Cyber crime and other forms of criminal activity that make use of our national computing infrastructure.

In fact the list of electronic based criminal activity includes such things as:

- Credit card theft
- Credit card fraud
- Bank account theft
- Breaking and entering into protected corporate and government databases and networks (hacking)
- Identity theft
- Harassment
- Fraud and con games
- Illegal gambling

Law enforcement has been ill equipped to deal with these criminal activities, but they are catching up. More resources need to be devoted to prevention and prosecution.

Most people would recognize all but two items on the above list as clearly criminal. The two activities that people sometimes view as inconsequential are illegal gambling and hacking.

Hacking, attempting to access networks, systems and databases by essentially breaking into them electronically, is illegal. But even before it was illegal, it was clearly unethical. In addition to being an electronic version of trespassing on private property, hacking jeopardizes confidential information, including personal identity information (social security numbers and credit card numbers, for example) that is clearly ethically off limits. Hacking can also bring down a network or a business application thereby costing the company money, damaged customer relationships, inability to process future business and in extreme cases legal problems with customers, clients, suppliers or others. You might as well walk into the company's office building and yell, "Fire!"

Spam

Spam is sending an e-mail advertisement out in large quantity to large numbers of e-mail addresses simultaneously. These e-mails frequently are totally unsolicited, are sometimes salacious in content, can contain computer viruses or other executable code that will harm your machine and/or cost you money. But primarily they are a nuisance at best and a productivity problem for employees. Spam is not currently against the law in all fifty states, but it is in a few. Many people are trying to create ways to block or filter spam, but so far with limited practical results.

Computer Viruses

Anything that deliberately damages another person's computer should be against the law. Virus creators are occasionally identified and prosecuted, but the primary defense continues to be regular virus scans with frequently updated software. Deliberately sending a virus is now illegal in many jurisdictions.

Chapter Thirteen – Individual Responsibility

Introduction

Throughout this book, we have examined the behavior of business either as an organization or as principally the behavior of management and executives. But all of us have a role to play, both in improving the level of integrity in our own company and in other companies and the nation at large.

Your Responsibility

Edmund Burke is often quoted as having said, "Evil triumphs when good men do nothing."

Sir Thomas Moore, who was put to death when he would not acknowledge one of Henry VIII's divorces as legitimate in the eyes of the Church, took the position that "Silence is consent."

There is no question that if all of us are quiet and do nothing when unethical behavior occurs, the likelihood of more unethical behavior will increase. Yet at the same time we often feel trapped, uninformed and ill suited to pass judgment on the behavior of our company, our colleagues or our management.

We may feel ill suited or ill equipped to challenge the behavior of others for a variety of reasons that have to do with the complexity of the situation, our ability to articulate our concerns, our ability to get management's attention or our personal credibility and voice with our colleagues and others. We may feel trapped because we are concerned that raising questions may impair our career or result in job loss. We may feel uninformed because we don't know what management's plans and strategies are until they have already been enacted.

There are some practical steps you can take to overcome some of these obstacles.

First, to overcome concerns about being ill equipped to analyze the situation and make an appropriate judgment you should take steps to make sure you have good information. Examining each of our Seven Layers will provide a guide to acquiring that knowledge.

1. Get to know the law. You don't have to be a lawyer to understand the basics of the law as it applies to or impacts your particular job. Make it a point to know which regulatory agencies of which levels of government are concerned with the tasks you perform. Find out what the basic laws are that apply to your activity and your particular job. The law is complex and there are times when people observe behavior, assume the other party knows what they are doing and accept it simply because they are not aware that it is illegal.

2. Ask for information about the company's contracts and agreements. If you are working on a project for a client, you should know what the contract says about what you are doing, how you are reporting your time and detailing expenses, what the deadlines are, how the work quality will be reviewed, what the customer's people are supposed to do to help you and much more. Don't be in the dark. Ask for appropriate details. You don't need to know the terms or even have a copy of the contract, but you should know what it is that you are obligated to provide to the customer as part of the agreement. Be sure to also know what things you can't do (offer a job to one of the customer's personnel, for example).

3. If you are a member of a profession, know your professional code of ethics and the rationale for them. If you are not a member of a profession, conduct yourself in a professional manner just the same. Remember that professionals:

   - Apply the most current knowledge and skills
   - Welcome assistance

- Are open to scrutiny
- Maintain objectivity
- Maintain independence
- Challenge errors that may become problems, even their own mistakes

4. Know the normal rules of doing business for your industry and in particular for your tasks in the industry. If you are a sales associate or account representative, get to know what the standard practices are for client entertainment, reimbursable travel expenses, appropriate ways to contact an account, what the typical sales cycle includes, how leads can be protected and much more. Knowing these standards will decrease your overall learning curve, keep you from getting at odds with colleagues and prospects and help you to recognize something that doesn't "smell" right.

5. When examining behavior you have concerns about, or in contemplating your own actions, don't forget to look outside your industry and profession to the broader communities involved. Ask how this action would look if it showed up in tomorrow's newspapers and cable news broadcasts. If the answer is that it would be embarrassing, then you probably should reconsider.

6. Be sure to maintain integrity in your personal relationships – at the office and outside of work. If you treat others with the respect that you want to be treated with yourself, you will earn a well-deserved reputation as a solid individual.

7. Take time, continually, to develop your spiritual life. Know what your values are, what you stand for and where the boundaries are for your own behavior. When someone asks you to do something you don't feel good about, make sure you know why it violates your personal moral and spiritual values and try to explain that to them. If your boundaries are violated consistently and frequently, look for a new assignment.

Second, if you are uninformed about what the company is doing, take reasonable steps to become informed. Management is not the only available source of information. Here are some others:

1. <u>The Internet</u>. If you were not an employee and were buying your company's stock you would do some basic research. Do the same on your employer. If the company is publicly held, you can get all the latest official SEC filings, request copies of its annual report, get copies of reports from various financial analysts, find the latest news clippings, and review its external Internet site.

2. <u>Other people in your industry</u>. You have personal contacts with suppliers, competitors, recruiters and others. Keep your ears open and pay attention to anything being said about what your company is doing. It may be rumor, or it may be factual. Stay tuned in.

3. <u>The company's internal employee information sources</u>. Don't skip the employee meetings. Watch the bulletin boards. Read the monthly newsletter.

4. <u>Your manager or supervisor</u>. If you want to know what the company's strategy is to beat the competition, ask. If you want to know how next year's earnings might be impacted by yesterday's big announcement, ask. Don't forget that some of what you hear may be confidential and not for outside disclosure. Be sure you know what is and isn't publicly available information.

5. <u>Your broker or other financial advisor</u>. Brokerage firms often have access to additional research reports and other analysis about publicly traded companies that you may not be able to get over the Internet. Get copies of these reports and read them.

Of course, if your company is small and/or privately held, you will have less access to external information. The burden is on you to keep your eyes and ears open and to ask questions when you have them.

Third, understand that when you feel trapped there are often ways out. Seek the advice of your spouse or a good friend. Examine some of the options. Here are some pointers.

1. Be sure you have the proper perspective. Many times people become upset with some condition at work that has nothing to do with ethical behavior. If that is the case, then your goals for resolution will take a different course, such as finding a new job assignment within the company, seeking an assignment with

another department or trying to take some training to improve your skills.

2. If the item is an ethical matter, again make sure you have it in perspective. Everyone is human and perfection is impossible to achieve. If this is a problem with a single individual's behavior, then it is not necessarily of the same magnitude as deliberately falsifying the company's earnings. Ask yourself if you are being called on to step outside of your own moral boundaries.

3. If you do have the right perspective and the problem is significant for the company and/or yourself, then some type of action is warranted. There are always options. You may be able to speak up on an anonymous basis to the company. You may have access to a particular manager or executive that has a good reputation. You may feel comfortable discussing the matter privately with an appropriate person. In some cases, the human resource department in your company may be able to help you. If it is a legal matter, consider presenting it to the corporate attorney.

If you can't trust any of the management, or human resources or even the company's internal counsel, then that should say something about the overall culture at the company. You may want to start looking for a new place to work.

Whistle Blowing

Whistle blowing is essentially raising a problem to the highest level of authority within the company (the CEO and / or the Board of Directors) or going outside the company (to a regulatory agency, law enforcement agency or the press) to expose a perceived problem. Whistle blowing is a very significant step and can easily become a career threatening move at both your current employer and with respect to anything you do in the future.

Whistle blowing presents legal problems as well. While there is legislation to protect whistle blowers in certain situations, you should definitely consult an attorney before taking this step.

Building Integrity in Your Company

For most of us, there is no immediate ethical crisis that requires significant action. Indeed, as pointed out elsewhere, the road to unethical corporate behavior is often one of minute steps taken on a day-to-day basis. These small steps are those that build a dysfunctional management culture in which the truth is afraid to come out or in which the negative side of otherwise desirable behavior, such as building revenue, becomes dominant.

Similarly, the road to ethical business behavior is usually paved with positive small bricks laid down day-to-day by people just like you. Here are some of them:

Personal Steps

1. Be educated and informed. As we discussed above, get all the knowledge you can about the relevant law, relevant contracts, industry norms and professional codes of ethics.

2. If you are not a member of a profession, act as though you are anyway.

3. Honor your personal relationships and commitments.

4. Give time to your spiritual growth, in whatever form you are comfortable with.

5. Know yourself and your own moral boundaries.

Steps with Your Work

1. Always do the best job you can. Don't be satisfied with mediocre results.

2. Take your job seriously when you are at the office, but keep it in perspective when you are at home.

3. Learn to work more efficiently and effectively. Efficiency is getting something done in less time; effectiveness is getting the right things done. Prioritize your activities, assignments and

tasks. Don't waste your time on things that are unimportant; spend quality time on important things so they will be of high quality.

4. Learn to delegate. It's called *leverage*. You are only one person and have only twenty-four hours in each day. By delegating to others, you can increase the number of things you achieve without increasing the number of hours you work. In addition, delegation gives others the opportunity to take on a new assignment and to learn how to do something new. It also gives their supervisor a chance to see first hand what their potential really is.

5. Don't be a worker or supervisor with an attitude. That's how a destructive, dysfunctional work environment starts. If you are a worker, give management a chance. They have their own personality problems to work out and learning to be a good manager is a process, not a result. If you are a supervisor, consider how to build trust and confidence in your team. Leadership is earned, not given, regardless of what title your management may have conveyed on you.

6. Praise people when they bring an important problem to your attention. Remember that if you scold a bird dog every time he brings you a bird, he will eventually stop retrieving.

7. Take action when you see something going on that you believe is wrong. Get the facts first, take some time (even if it is only two very deliberate seconds) to assess the best thing to do, and then give it attention. Long-term problems arise when inappropriate behavior is allowed to happen every day without being corrected.

8. Never forget that Americans are very peer group oriented. Your co-workers and colleagues are influenced by your behavior, even if you don't realize it.

9. If you are a supervisor, expect a lot from your team. Challenge them to do better, but do it in a positive way. Don't expect them to improve without some level of feedback, informal training and review. Recognize their accomplishments personally by taking time out to acknowledge good results.

10. A company with high morale is a fertile ground for ethical business behavior. A company with low morale and a dysfunctional culture is fertile ground for unethical behavior to occur and be accepted. Know how to build morale in your organization. Better pay alone will not achieve high morale. People want to know that their work and contribution is appreciated and that their job is important. The fastest way to low morale is to make people feel unappreciated and unrecognized. Resolve today to recognize and appreciate someone else's good efforts.

Following these simple and straightforward recommendations will help you to do your part to improve business practices and ethics. Set a high standard and work accordingly; over time you will become a positive example for others and a contributor to ethical behavior in your part of the organization.

Chapter Fourteen – Conclusion

The subject of business ethics is vast and detailed examples of unethical behavior are endless. The underlying law is complex and fills entire bookshelves. Rather than attempt to cover all that someone needs to know, our objective has been to give you some tools, practical advice and a broad overview of the law so that you have a basis to move forward and become capable of reaching your own decisions.

At the risk of being accused of moral relativism, we have presented you with seven perspectives on integrity and ethics as part of your tool kit. Although spiritual and moral values are the ultimate foundation of ethical behavior, we have started from the pinnacle of our foundation diagram – the law – as the one point we are most likely to all agree on. Obeying the law, and the selfish reasons for doing so, was our first perspective on ethical business behavior.

Each subsequent Layer has taken us further away from consensus and detail, further away from an existing shared societal measurement process (our legal system), and closer to an ideal whose details are limited and may easily differ from one person to another. Yet that ideal, our individual spiritual and moral values, is the ultimate guide for each of us in making judgments about our behavior and that of others in the business community.

We should be careful not to confuse ethics with the law. Obeying the law is a key element of good business ethics, but it is not the only element. Business must recognize that its contracts and agreements with others are an extension of the law and should be followed until the parties involved formally agree to a change. Business must recognize that it exists in an industry with other players and that our underlying capitalist and democratic system works best when competition is not only intensely innovative, but fair to all. Professionals in our business community should be ever mindful of the guidelines of their professions.

Business must continue to recognize that it exists within a community of people – geographic, political and social – and that its actions and behavior have the potential for broad and devastating impact on our country, our physical environment, our economy and the lives of people it has never met. Ethical business behavior must go beyond what the law requires and seek to balance profit with the betterment of our way of life.

Personal relationships, both business and family, should be honored. People are not disposable elements in any system that values ethical behavior. Employees need training and encouragement, not recrimination and intimidation. Building a positive culture ultimately has a long lasting impact on the bottom line of any company.

Finally, ethics of any kind are based on what people believe is best for themselves, their families, the nation and the human race as a whole. Those values, while individualized for each of us, do not spring from a vacuum. They are rooted in an evolving sense of how we should best treat each other and what our role is in the universe. For some people, that foundation starts with their religious and moral upbringing. For others, it has been found as a result of their own circuitous journey through life. And for some, spiritual values are an untapped resource, perhaps not yet even visible on their horizon.

The challenge of business ethics is to moderate between the minimal requirement of obeying the law and the ultimate ideal that not everyone has bought into. We struggle to move forward, then go through a period such as the one at the beginning of this millennium in which our conduct of business and our view of business takes giant backward steps. Such forward lurches and backward failings are the history of the human race.

About the Authors

George P. Jones, a management consultant and co-founder of ChangeMakers, Inc., provides ethics training and consulting. He began his career at Arthur Andersen & Co.'s Houston office in the division that later became Accenture. Becoming a partner in Andersen in 1985, he specialized in technology and financial services. He twice had responsibility for developing new training programs for Andersen, including a replacement for the firm's three-week new hire training program that was deployed around the world.

Following Andersen, Mr. Jones was in charge of the Chicago and Houston operations of BSG, a start up systems integrator, where he was responsible for over 120 consultants. In Chicago, Mr. Jones was responsible for developing all aspects of a new operation. After returning to Houston he led the 120 employees of BSG's original office through a period of significant change, culminating in BSG's acquisition by a publicly traded company. He received an M.S. degree in Computer Science from The Ohio State University and is a CPA in the State of Texas.

Currently a faculty member at Rice University, June Ferrill, Ph.D., teaches business ethics, ethical decision-making for engineers, entrepreneurial communications and managerial communications. Dr. Ferrill has given training for and consulted with Bank of America, Continental Airlines, Ernst & Young, Halliburton, and Arthur Andersen, among others. She served as Communications Consultant at McKinsey & Company, assisting project teams in developing client communications for Fortune 500 companies.

After McKinsey, Dr. Ferrill played a significant role as training development specialist for KBR's Engineering Division, a Halliburton subsidiary. She developed on-going training in communications, management development, quality control, team building, and strategic planning. She was an editor and contributing author to *Business and Managerial Communications: New Perspectives*, an 800-page college textbook. She has a Ph.D. in the Joint Ph.D. Program in English and Education, University of Michigan.